complete
thai
cooking

complete thai cooking

hamlyn

First published in Great Britain in 2006 by
Hamlyn, a division of Octopus Publishing Group Ltd
2–4 Heron Quays, London E14 4JP

Copyright © Octopus Publishing Group Ltd 2006

Distributed in the United States and Canada by
Sterling Publishing Co., Inc.
387 Park Avenue South, New York, NY 10016-8810

ISBN-13: 978-0-600-61574-3
ISBN-10: 0-600-61574-X

A CIP catalogue record for this book is available from the British
Library

Printed and bound in China

10 9 8 7 6 5 4 3

Notes

Standard level spoon and cup measurements are used in all recipes.

Eggs should be large unless otherwise stated. The Department of Health and Human Services advises that eggs should not be consumed raw. This book contains dishes made with raw or lightly cooked eggs. It is prudent for more vulnerable people such as pregnant and nursing mothers, invalids, the elderly, babies, and young children to avoid uncooked or lightly cooked dishes made with eggs. Once prepared, these dishes should be kept refrigerated and used promptly.

Milk should be whole milk unless otherwise stated.

This book includes dishes made with nuts and nut derivatives. It is advisable for customers with known allergic reactions to nuts and nut derivatives and those who may be potentially vulnerable to these allergies such as pregnant and nursing mothers, invalids, the elderly, babies, and children to avoid dishes made with nuts and nut oils. It is also prudent to check the labels of pre-prepared ingredients for the possible inclusion of nut derivatives.

Pepper should be freshly ground black pepper unless otherwise stated.

Fresh herbs should be used, unless otherwise stated. If unavailable, use dried herbs as an alternative, but halve the quantities stated.

Ovens should be preheated to the specified temperature—if using a fan-assisted oven, follow the manufacturer's instructions for adjusting the time and the temperature.

Contents

Introduction

Thailand is a beautiful and fertile country, which produces some of the best food in the world, and there can be no doubt about the importance of good food to its people. From the moment you set foot in the country, your senses are assailed from all sides by the smells of delicious chicken and dried squid and of pungent spices and herbs, the sound of pestles thudding into mortars and cleavers chopping vegetables, and the sight of exotic fruits loaded onto stalls, while out of the corner of your eye you see a huge whoosh of flame reaching up around a wok and the cook laughing at your surprise.

The beauty of Thai food lies in its contrasts—hot, cool, sour, sweet, crunchy, soft, all with a wonderful citrus tang —and Thai cuisine and its ingredients have had a considerable impact on our own food in recent years. Greatly increased numbers of visitors to Thailand have been discovering for themselves the particular delights of Thailand's unique cuisine, and more and more Thais have been leaving home to set up restaurants all over the world, from Sydney to London, and Auckland to San Francisco.

Thailand is still overwhelmingly an agricultural country, and its major natural resource is its agricultural potential. Although the agricultural sector's contribution to the national GNP has declined considerably in the last 40 years because of the huge growth in manufacturing output, the food industry still employs two-thirds of the labor force and directly supports 60 percent of the population. The good thing about countries like Thailand, where the agriculture is still largely unintensive, is the fabulous quality of what is produced.

Whether at home or in countries far away, Thais always base their cooking on fresh ingredients, and wherever they are they remain true to a typical Thai style; there is no compromising on authentic Thai recipes to suit the palates of the countries where their cooks happen to be. The importance of preparation and cooking of food in Thailand is one of the first things you notice on arrival there. Everyone appreciates good food, and there are restaurants and food stalls everywhere you look. Thailand's tropical monsoon climate is responsible for the abundance of fruit and vegetables, which includes varieties of everything we grow in the West and many, many more.

Thailand's geographical position at the heart of Southeast Asia means that its cooking has taken on and adapted to its own character and preferences the cuisines of countries around it, notably China and India, but also Malaysia and Indonesia. In addition, European traders seeking spices and other goods have influenced Thai cooking, and it was, in fact, the Portuguese who introduced the chili to Thailand in the early 16th century. Today, the chili is one of the most important ingredients in Thai cuisine. Cardamoms came from India by way of Burma, coriander and cumin arrived from the Middle East, tapioca from Central America and tomatoes from South America via Europe.

Thai cooking is not a pale imitation of other Asian styles, however. There are plenty of hot dishes, and cooks make great use of the Chinese wok, although Thai stir-fries tend to be lighter and more highly spiced than Chinese ones. Thai stir-fries are also free of the cornstarch often used by the Chinese as a thickening agent.

The curries have a greater lightness of touch than those of India, allied to an aromatic sourness and a certain sweetness that is uniquely Thai. The basic ingredients of a Thai curry, which may be pork, beef, chicken, or fish, or simple fresh vegetables, are cut into more delicate slivers than the chunks that are usual in Indian cooking, and the fiery taste comes from the pastes—red curry paste based on red chilies and green curry paste on green ones—that flavor them.

With the curry pastes are added fresh herbs, spices, and other flavorings, which may include lemon grass, cilantro (the leaves, stalks, and root of fresh cilantro are all used in Thai cooking), lime leaves, three types of basil, galangal, ginger, garlic, and shallots.

Healthy eating

Over the last few years, we have all become increasingly aware of how food impacts on our health and the ways in which large-scale, industrialized food production affects our environment, often in terrible ways. More and more of us want to eat free-range eggs and organically grown vegetables. We are aware of the importance of eating locally produced, seasonally available foods that have not traveled halfway round the world to our stores. We are also increasingly aware of problems with pesticides, with nitrates in the water table, and with our water supplies in general. We have begun to buy eco-friendly cleaning materials and washing powders, we recycle paper and bottles, and we all want to live a life that is better for us and better for our planet. Cooking and eating Thai food is a delicious and unusual way of eating healthily.

The Thai diet is one of the healthiest in the world. There are plenty of fresh vegetables and fruit, good-quality rice and noodles, and relatively small amounts of meat and fish. Dairy products are virtually unused by most Thai people, and cattle raising is on a small scale.

You are more likely to find pigs, chickens, and ducks on farms and smallholdings than cattle, and this is reflected in the cooking.

The food includes several types of fruit and vegetables that are not regularly used in the West but that offer a surprising range of nutrients. Limes are a good source of vitamin C, and bean sprouts continue to grow and form nutrients after picking, unlike most other vegetables. A normal helping of mung bean sprouts provides about 75 percent of the adult RDA of vitamin C and is also a good source of some of the B vitamins. Garlic helps to lower cholesterol and blood pressure. It also has antiviral and antibacterial properties. Papaya is not only a good source of vitamin C and betacarotene but also provides small amounts of calcium and iron as well. The juice contains papain, an enzyme similar to pepsin, which is produced by our digestive systems to break down proteins. Papain is very good for combating digestive disorders; indeed, the food industry uses papain as a natural meat tenderizer.

Thai cuisine

Thai eating is usually very relaxed, with six or eight dishes appearing in the center of the table and everyone helping themselves to a small amount of each. There is always a big bowl of rice, which is so important to Thai people that their verb "to eat" is literally "eat rice." In the northern, mountainous regions of Thailand, people eat a mountain rice, which does not require flooded paddy fields in which to grow. This rice is of poor quality, both in flavor and nutritionally. Sticky (glutinous) rice, which is short-grained, is the staple in the rest of northern and northeastern Thailand. The cuisine there is much drier. People use their fingers to eat with, making little balls of rice between their fingers and thumb and using these to scoop up the rest of the food. In central and southern

Thailand, sticky rice is mainly used in desserts. Although Thais like sweet things and make many dessert-type dishes, they actually eat them as snacks rather than at the end of the meal.

Fish is important in the Thai diet and always has been. The whole country is crossed by rivers and natural waterways, so freshwater fish and shellfish are readily available in places where fish from the sea is unobtainable. Much fish of all types is dried, salted, or turned into shrimp paste or nam pla (fish sauce).

Forks and spoons are the usual implements with which to eat, unless the dish is noodles or a noodle soup, in which case chopsticks and a spoon are used. This use of chopsticks shows the influence of China, which goes back to the first century AD when the tribal T'ai people began to migrate from China down to Burma, Laos, Vietnam, and Thailand. Here they joined other tribal people, whose main influences were Burmese and Cambodian, themselves both influenced by India. Over the next few centuries, first one and then another power waxed and waned, then in the 13th century the Kingdom of Sukhothai was formed. All the tribes absorbed ideas and languages from one another and gradually became a cohesive people in their own right. They were called Siamese, and the country became known as Siam. That name was officially changed to Thailand in 1949. All these influences were responsible for what we now know as Thai cuisine, and help to explain how it came to be as immensely varied and unique as it is.

There are not many vegetarian Thais, but their numbers are growing. One of Thailand's greatest sources of foreign exchange is the tourist trade and significant numbers of Western tourists are vegetarians, so it is now becoming quite easy to find wonderful and unusual

Dining Thai-style is an informal affair, with several different dishes served at about the same time, to which everyone helps themselves.

vegetarian food in Thailand. Specifically vegetarian food stalls exist in many markets, as does the occasional vegetarian restaurant. In addition, if you do not see what you want on a menu in a non-vegetarian restaurant, the chef will usually be happy to cook a vegetarian dish for you if you ask. You will find that the more you try to cook vegetarian Thai food, the quicker and easier it will be, and the more adventurous you will become.

Getting started

If you are thinking of experimenting with Thai food, your first step should be to visit a specialty Asian food store or market. Here you will be able to buy everything you need, in both food and equipment terms. Although many supermarkets and stores carry some useful items, such as noodles, bamboo shoots, and soy sauce, they cannot compete with the real thing. For example, Thai jasmine or fragrant rice can be bought in large sacks from Asian stores, and these will last a long time and will be considerably cheaper than buying the rice in individual boxes or small bags.

Cooking Thai-style may seem a little alarming at first. So many small amounts of different things go into each dish, and somehow a number of different dishes have to be ready to eat at more or less the same time. The answer is to choose your menu carefully. Rice can be reheated easily in a steamer, and curries can also be cooked in advance and reheated. Soup can be cooked in a saucepan, leaving the wok free for deep-frying a fish or stir-frying, and salads can be prepared in advance and finished at the last moment.

As with any other form of cooking, the more often you do it the easier it becomes, until you find you can turn out inexpensive, nutritious meals at the drop of a hat.

Whether or not you become totally addicted to Thai food, you can be sure that when you prepare a Thai meal you will be eating healthily and enjoyably.

Equipment

Thai kitchens are extremely simple compared to the ones we are used to in the West, and it's probable that you will already have most of the equipment required to cook Thai food. The whole experience of Thai cooking is hands-on—there is lots of chopping and pounding and tearing, but most Thais do not have ovens, so they have not evolved the sort of long, slow casserole cooking or roasting that are features of Western cooking.

You will find a heavy kitchen cleaver useful for peeling (when you hold the blade held horizontally) or chopping vegetables, cutting through bones, opening pineapples and coconuts, and finely chopping herbs (when you can use the whole blade), and don't forget a good-quality cutting board. Of course, you can also use kitchen knives, vegetable peelers, and scissors equally well.

A bamboo-handled wire basket is useful for blanching vegetables, plunging noodles into stock or boiling water for a few moments to cook, and for removing deep-fried food from the hot oil, although a slotted spoon does this last task perfectly well. A long-handled spatula, shaped rather like a shovel, is ideal for moving the ingredients around while you are stir-frying.

Wok

You will need a wok, preferably one with a wooden handle; some of the cheaper woks have metal handles, and you can burn yourself if you aren't careful. If you do not have a wok, you could use a large, nonstick skillet. The advantage of a wok is the way the whole surface heats up, the hottest part being in the center, allowing you to push ingredients to the side if you think they are almost done and to cook something else in the center. Woks are also deep enough to hold plenty of liquid, so you can cook curries and deep-fry in them, as well as stir-fry.

Thai food is cooked fast. The ingredients are chopped into small pieces before you begin and cooked for a short time over a fairly high heat. They should all be slightly crunchy when they reach your mouth. Thai cooks work over a very high flame, very fast, and lift the wok off the flame when they want to reduce the temperature. When you first try cooking in a wok, a moderately high temperature will do; it will allow you to concentrate on the cooking and not waste precious moments adjusting the heat.

When you stir-fry, it is best to heat the wok, add a little oil, swirl it around and get it good and hot before you add your first ingredients. Think carefully about exactly what it is you are cooking and the order in which the ingredients should be added. Put more solid items, such as carrots and broccoli stalks, into the wok first, with the most delicate vegetables, such as small leaves or bean sprouts, which are cooked for just a few seconds, going in last. Don't be afraid to toss the food around in the wok; you need to keep moving it from the center to the side and back again.

Steamer

You will also need a steamer, either a stainless steel one, which you will find very useful in your everyday cooking too, or a bamboo steamer of the kind you can find in Asian markets. You can rig up your own steamer easily enough by putting a metal colander over a saucepan of

boiling water. Line the colander with cheesecloth if you want to steam rice, if you don't have an electric rice steamer. You can steam dumplings on a plate placed in the colander with a lid on top to trap the steam. Make sure that the water in the saucepan does not dry out.

The advantage of a bamboo steamer is that the steam does not condense on the lid and drip moisture onto the food below, which can spoil its appearance. If you are cooking something like a whole fish in a metal steamer, cover it with paper towels to protect it.

Food to be steamed is often wrapped in leaves, usually banana leaves, which not only imparts the flavor of the leaf to the food, but looks appealing when the food is brought to the table.

Mortar and pestle

If you want to produce curry pastes and sauces with an authentic texture, you will need a large mortar and pestle to blend chilies, garlic, onions, and other spices together. However, you can use an electric food processor to good effect; indeed, many urban Thais use them these days. If you want to grind fresh, whole spices but don't have a mortar and pestle, you can use an electric coffee grinder, thoroughly cleaned both before and after use, or a spice grinder. If you are going to grind fresh spices on a regular basis, it would be worth buying either a mortar and pestle or a coffee grinder or spice grinder specifically for this purpose.

A large mortar and pestle is a must for pounding and grinding herbs and spices. Choose a heavy stoneware or marble variety.

Basic Recipes

At the heart of Thai cooking lie vitally important curry pastes and good stocks. The stocks and pastes described here are ideal for using in the recipes in this book.

Red Curry Paste

6 dried red chilies, seeded, soaked, drained, and roughly chopped

2 tablespoons chopped lemon grass or ¼ teaspoon grated lemon zest

1 teaspoon chopped cilantro root or stalk

1 tablespoon chopped shallots

1 tablespoon chopped garlic

1 teaspoon chopped fresh galangal or gingerroot

2 teaspoons coriander seeds

1 teaspoon cumin seeds

6 white peppercorns

1 teaspoon salt

1 teaspoon shrimp paste

put all the ingredients in a food processor and process to a thick paste.

alternatively, put the chilies in a mortar and pound with a pestle, then add the lemon grass or lemon zest and pound it with the fresh cilantro, and so on with all the remaining ingredients.

transfer the paste to an airtight container. Any that you do not use immediately may be stored in the refrigerator for up to 3 weeks.

Preparation time: *15 minutes*

Yellow Curry Paste

3 small fresh chilies (yellow or orange)

4 garlic cloves, halved

4 shallots, roughly chopped

3 teaspoons ground turmeric

I teaspoon salt

I5 black peppercorns

I lemon grass stalk, chopped

I inch piece of fresh gingerroot, peeled and chopped

put all the ingredients in a food processor and process to a thick paste.

alternatively, pound all the ingredients together in a mortar with a pestle.

transfer the paste to an airtight container. Any that you do not use immediately may be stored in the refrigerator for up to 3 weeks.

Preparation time: *15 minutes*

Green Curry Paste

I5 small fresh green chilies

4 garlic cloves, halved

2 lemon grass stalks, finely chopped, or ¼ teaspoon grated lemon zest

2 kaffir lime leaves, torn

2 shallots, chopped

I cup cilantro leaves, stalks, and roots

I inch piece of fresh gingerroot, peeled and chopped

2 teaspoons coriander seeds

I teaspoon black peppercorns

I teaspoon finely grated lime zest

½ teaspoon salt

2 tablespoons peanut oil

put all the ingredients in a food processor and process to a thick paste.

alternatively, put the chilies in a mortar and pound with a pestle, then add the garlic and pound it with the lemon grass or lemon zest, and so on with all the remaining ingredients, then mix in the oil with a spoon.

transfer the paste to an airtight container. Any that you do not use immediately may be stored in the refrigerator for up to 3 weeks.

Preparation time: *15 minutes*

Chicken Stock

3½ lb whole chicken

1 lb chicken giblets

1 onion, halved

1 carrot, roughly chopped

2 celery sticks, including leaves, roughly chopped

7½ cups cold water

2 garlic cloves

1 lemon grass stalk, roughly chopped, or ¼ teaspoon grated lemon zest

1 kaffir lime leaf

10 black peppercorns

3 large fresh red chilies

put the chicken in a large, heavy saucepan or casserole with the giblets, onion, carrot, and celery and pour over the measurement water until the ingredients are just covered. Put the pan over a very low heat and bring it to a boil as slowly as possible. Reduce the heat and simmer for about 50 minutes. When the liquid begins to simmer, remove the scum that rises to the surface until only white foam rises.

add all the remaining ingredients, cover, and simmer gently for 2 hours. Use a heat diffuser if you need to.

remove the chicken and set aside for another use. Strain the stock without pressing the juices from the vegetables—this helps to keep it clear. Use as much as you need immediately, quickly cooling and freezing the remainder for future use.

Makes about 6 cups
Preparation time: *5 minutes*
Cooking time: *about 3 hours*

Beef Stock

7½ cups cold water

12 oz beef or veal bones with some meat on, roughly chopped

1 carrot, roughly chopped

1 celery stick, roughly chopped

1 onion, quartered

1 inch piece of fresh gingerroot, peeled and sliced

2 cilantro plants, including roots

5 black peppercorns, crushed

put all the ingredients in a large saucepan and bring to a boil. Reduce the heat and simmer for 1½ hours. From time to time skim off any fat that rises to the surface.

strain the stock into a clean bowl, discard the solids and other unwanted parts and allow to cool.

cover the stock and leave in the refrigerator for 4–5 hours or overnight. Remove any fat that has solidified on the surface.

Makes about 4 cups
Preparation time: *10 minutes, plus cooling and chilling*
Cooking time: *about 1½ hours*

Vegetable Stock

2 large onions, quartered

4 large fresh red chilies

2 carrots (about 8 oz), halved

¼ small white cabbage, halved

1 small head of celery, including leaves, chopped

1 cup cilantro leaves, stalks, and roots

½ cup basil leaves and stalks

½ head of Chinese cabbage, chopped

½ mooli or 6 radishes, peeled

25 black peppercorns

½ teaspoon salt

1 teaspoon palm sugar or light brown sugar

8 cups water

put all the ingredients in a heavy saucepan or casserole. Bring to a boil, then reduce the heat, cover, and simmer for 1 hour.

remove the lid and boil hard for 10 minutes. Allow the stock to cool, then strain. Use as much as you need immediately, quickly cooling and freezing the remainder for future use.

Makes about 7½ cups
Preparation time: *5–10 minutes, plus cooling*
Cooking time: *about 1¼ hours*

Fish Stock

1 lb raw white fish heads and bones, and shrimp heads and shells, if available

10 cups cold water

3 shallots

1 celery stick, including leaves, roughly chopped

1 kaffir lime leaf

½ lemon grass stalk or ¼ teaspoon grated lemon zest

2 garlic cloves

½ cup cilantro stalks and roots

put the fish trimmings and measurement water into a large, heavy saucepan and bring to a boil. Skim off any scum that rises to the surface.

add the shallots, celery, lime leaf, lemon grass or lemon zest, garlic, and cilantro, cover, and simmer for 50 minutes.

strain the stock and use as much as you need immediately, quickly cooling and freezing the remainder for future use.

Makes about 8 cups
Preparation time: *5 minutes*
Cooking time: *about 1 hour*

Cook's Terms

As Thai cuisine has gained in popularity outside Thailand, first Asian markets, then supermarkets, and now many small, local stores sell an increasing range of Thai ingredients. Most of the ingredients used in this book are readily available, but alternatives are included for the more unusual items wherever possible. It is worth paying a little extra for your ingredients to make sure that they taste as good as they should.

Asian greens

Thai cooks use many different green vegetables, including bok choy, choy sum, and Chinese cabbage. Chinese broccoli is available fresh at Asian markets. It is similar to European sprouting broccoli except that it is longer and thinner, with more stalk and less floret. The stalk is the most interesting part, and it is sliced and cooked in many ways.

Bamboo shoots

The young, ivory-colored, conical-shaped shoots of edible bamboo plants are tender and crunchy, and add texture and sweetness to many dishes. Bamboo shoots are available canned, fresh, and sometimes vacuum-packed.

Banana leaves

These can be found in Asian markets and are used to contain food during steaming and broiling. You can use foil or small bowls, depending on your needs, but banana leaves are more authentic and look spectacular. They also impart a faint flavor.

Basil

Holy basil is used as often as sweet (European) basil in Thai cookery. With smaller, darker leaves and purple stalks, it is less sweet than European basil, which may be used instead.

Bean sauce

Black, yellow, and red bean sauces made from preserved soybeans are available in jars. Black beans are available in cans and bags and should be rinsed and chopped before use. Unused beans and their liquid can be stored indefinitely if kept in a sealed container in the refrigerator. Bean sauce and beans can be bought from most supermarkets and Asian markets.

Bitter melon

This has a fairly pale green, lumpy skin and is found in Asian markets. It has a very bitter taste, but you can use zucchini or cucumber if you prefer.

Chilies

There are so many different kinds of chili that it would be difficult to list them all. As a rule, the smaller the chili the fiercer the heat, and red chilies are slightly less fierce because they become sweeter as they ripen. Most of the heat of chilies is contained in and around the seeds and the inner membrane. Thai cooks often include the seeds, but you may prefer to remove them for a milder flavor. Fresh orange and yellow chilies are often used in Thai cooking as much for their pretty colors as for their flavor. You can occasionally buy them from specialty

Asian stores and markets, but otherwise use whatever color you can get. See also page 148.

Cilantro

An essential ingredient in Thai cooking. All of the herb is used—the leaves, stalks, and roots. Roots can be stored in an airtight container in the refrigerator or freezer.

Coconut milk and cream

These are widely available in cans, packages, and blocks (which require added water). You can make coconut milk yourself from shredded coconut: place 2 cups coconut in a food processor or blender with 1¼ cups hand-hot water; blend for 30 seconds and strain the liquid through cheesecloth, squeezing it as dry as you can. This will produce thick coconut milk. If you repeat the process, then mix the two extractions, you will get a medium-thick coconut milk, suitable for most dishes. If you put this milk in the refrigerator, the "cream" will rise to the surface and can be taken off. Coconut milk lasts only 1–2 days, even in the refrigerator. If you are using coconut cream, stir it constantly while cooking because it curdles easily.

Curry paste

Ready-made pastes are available in jars and packages, or make your own (see pages 12–13). They freeze perfectly.

Egg roll skins

White and flimsy, these are made from flour and water and are usually square. Buy them ready-made, fresh or frozen in plastic bags, from Asian markets. They are fragile, so handle them gently. If you can't find the shape you need for a recipe, buy whatever you can and cut to the required shape. If you cannot find them, use sheets of phyllo pastry and cut them to size.

Fragrant rice

The main rice of Thailand is jasmine rice or Thai fragrant rice. If Thai fragrant rice is not available, any good-quality long-grain rice, especially basmati, would suit the recipes in this book very well.

Galangal

This is a root similar to ginger, but the skin is thinner and slightly pink, and the taste is milder. It is available in some supermarkets and in Asian markets. It is peeled before use, then either sliced or chopped according to the recipe. Dried slices are also available, and 1 dried slice is the equivalent of ½ inch of the fresh root.

Garlic

White garlic is a main ingredient in Thai cooking and is used in many dishes. The size of the clove doesn't really affect the flavor, although the largest cloves are milder.

Ginger

Fresh gingerroot is readily available. Use it in the same way as galangal, as described above.

Lemon grass is one of the most popular herbs of Southeast Asia and is a vital flavor in Thai curry pastes.

Krachai

Also called lesser ginger, this root is smaller and fiercer than ginger and galangal, but it comes from the same family and should be treated in the same way. It is usually available dried in packages.

Lemon grass

Widely available from supermarkets in bundles of 4–6 stalks, the straw-like tops should be trimmed as well as the ends, and the stalks thinly sliced. If you can't get fresh lemon grass, dried and ground lemon grass is available, or you can use lemon zest or juice instead.

Limes and lime leaves

The type of lime grown in Thailand is called kaffir. Kaffir lime leaves can be bought fresh or dried in Asian

Nam pla (fish sauce) is a clear brown liquid, famous for its pungent aroma and strong, salty flavor.

markets and some supermarkets, but if you cannot find them, use lime zest or juice.

Mushrooms

Several types of mushroom are used in Thai dishes. Dried black fungus (cloud ear, mouse ear, or wood fungus) can be found in packages in Asian markets. Soak them in warm water for 15–20 minutes and drain them before use. Oyster mushrooms are available fresh from most supermarkets. Shiitake mushrooms can be found dried in Asian markets, health food stores, and some supermarkets, which also sell them fresh occasionally. If dried, they should be soaked in warm water for 15–20 minutes before use, then the hard stalk cut away and added to the stockpot. Shiitake are expensive, but you only need to use a few at a time. Straw mushrooms can be found in cans from supermarkets. Button, chestnut, and field mushrooms can be used if none of the other types are available.

Nam pla (fish sauce)

This essential ingredient in Thai cooking is widely available in supermarkets. It is a clear brown liquid, sold in bottles, made from pulverized, fermented, salted fish (usually anchovies). It has a strong flavor and pungent aroma. Although it is a contradiction in terms, there is a vegetarian "fish" sauce, which is sometimes available in large Asian markets or vegetarian stores. If you cannot find it, use light soy sauce or salt.

Noodles

Many kinds of noodle are used in Thai cooking, but the most commonly available are egg noodles, rice vermicelli, rice sticks, and glass noodles. Egg noodles can be bought fresh from Asian markets, but the dried ones, which are widely available at supermarkets, are just as good. Rice vermicelli are very thin, white, and translucent. Rice sticks are the same as vermicelli, only wider and flatter and available in varying widths. Glass noodles, also known as cellophane noodles, bean thread noodles, and bean vermicelli, are similar to rice vermicelli but are made from mung beans.

Palm sugar

This soft, raw light brown sugar is widely used in Southeast Asia. In Thailand it is often sold wet, giving it a thick, honey-like consistency, but it is exported in hard blocks, which can be broken into pieces and dissolved. It tastes delicious and is attractive in desserts. If you can't get it, use a light brown or Indian jaggery sugar.

Papaya

Also called pawpaw, this tropical fruit is available from supermarkets. When unripe, the pale green, slightly bitter flesh is used in salads. The orange flesh of ripe papaya tastes best with a little lime juice.

Shrimp paste

Available "fresh" or dried in tubs or wrapped blocks, this pungent ingredient is made of salted, decomposed shrimp. Dried blocks are stronger than the "fresh" variety. Shrimp paste is available from Asian markets.

Soy sauce

Soy sauce is made from fermented soybeans. Light soy sauce is used in the recipes in this book, unless otherwise indicated. Dark soy sauce is not only darker in color but is also thicker and slightly sweeter than light soy sauce.

Sticky rice

A type of short-grain rice, sometimes called glutinous rice, that is used in many Thai desserts. It is opaque and must be steamed. For best results, always soak for several hours or even overnight before cooking.

Tamarind

Dried tamarind pulp can be found in Chinese and Asian food stores. To make tamarind water, simmer the pulp for 2–3 minutes, allow to cool, then squeeze out the juice and discard the pulp and seeds. Tamarind concentrate can be bought in tubs; dissolve a spoonful in hot water. You can substitute lemon juice.

Tofu

There are several kinds of tofu (beancurd), which is made from soybeans. Fresh white tofu is sold in blocks in its own liquid. It is very delicate and will break up if stirred too much. Blocks of ready-fried tofu are much more solid. They are ideal for stir-frying. You can buy fairly solid white tofu cakes packed in water in plastic containers; these can be used for stir-frying if you can't get the ready-fried kind. All of these products are available from health food stores, supermarkets, and Asian markets.

Turmeric

This spice is a golden-yellow colorant with a mild flavor. It can sometimes be found fresh in Asian markets but is most often used in its dried, ground form.

Vinegar

It is worth looking for white rice vinegar or distilled white vinegar in large supermarkets or Asian markets. Cider vinegar is an acceptable alternative, but do not use malt vinegar, which does not suit Asian food.

Won ton skins

Made from flour and eggs, these are deep yellow or golden-brown in color. They are sold ready-made, fresh or frozen, in plastic bags from Asian markets. If a recipe uses differently shaped skins, cut them to shape with scissors. Alternatively, use sheets of phyllo pastry cut to the required shape.

Snacks and Appetizers

Crispy Wrapped Shrimp

Egg roll skins are widely available in Asian markets. They are delicate, so handle them gently and carefully cut them to size if you can only find larger ones.

3 oz ground pork

4 raw shrimp, peeled and finely chopped, plus 12 raw whole shrimp, unpeeled

½ teaspoon palm sugar or light brown sugar

¼ onion, finely chopped

1 garlic clove, finely chopped

2 teaspoons soy sauce

12 egg roll skins, each about 5 inches square

egg white, beaten, for sealing

about 3 cups oil, for deep-frying

basil or cilantro sprigs, to garnish

To serve

lime wedges

Hot Sweet Sauce (see page 246)

mix together the pork, chopped shrimp, sugar, onion, garlic, and soy sauce in a bowl.

peel the 12 whole shrimp, leaving the shell on the tails intact, and carefully cut open, making sure that you do not cut right through them.

put 1–2 teaspoons of the pork and shrimp mixture on to each opened prawn. Spread out an egg roll skin on a work surface and pull one corner about three-quarters of the way toward the opposite corner. Place a shrimp on the double thickness of the skin, leaving the tail free, and roll it up, tucking the ends in and sealing with a little egg white. Repeat until all the shrimp are wrapped.

heat the oil in a wok or deep skillet to 350–375°F, or until a cube of bread browns in 30 seconds. Deep-fry the shrimp rolls, in 2 batches if necessary, for about 5 minutes, or until golden brown. Remove with a slotted spoon and drain on paper towels. Garnish with basil or cilantro sprigs and serve with lime wedges and the hot sweet sauce.

Serves 4
Preparation time: *10–15 minutes*
Cooking time: *5–10 minutes*

Chicken Satay

Satay (or satei) sauce arrived in Thailand from Indonesia and often accompanies pork and beef as well as chicken. Use peanuts in the sauce for an authentic flavor.

1 lb boneless, skinless chicken breast, cut into 1–2 inch pieces

Marinade

1 tablespoon ground cinnamon

1 tablespoon ground cumin

1 teaspoon pepper

²⁄₃ cup peanut oil

½ cup soy sauce

2 tablespoons palm sugar or light brown sugar

Satay sauce

1 heaping teaspoon Red Curry Paste (see page 12)

1 tablespoon peanut oil

1 cup coconut milk

¼ cup palm sugar or light brown sugar

1½ tablespoons nam pla (fish sauce)

juice of 1 lime

½ cup Crushed Roasted Nuts—use peanuts (see page 248)

1 teaspoon crushed dried chilies

To garnish

roughly chopped onion

cucumber chunks

make the marinade. Mix all the marinade ingredients together in a bowl. Add the chicken pieces and turn in the marinade to coat thoroughly. Cover and allow to marinate in the refrigerator for at least 4 hours, preferably overnight, stirring occasionally.

make the satay sauce. Put the curry paste in a saucepan with the oil and stir over a low heat for 1 minute. Add the remaining sauce ingredients and cook over a moderate heat until thickened and blended. Remove from the heat, turn the sauce into a serving bowl and allow to cool.

carefully thread the chicken pieces onto bamboo skewers, presoaked in cold water for 1 hour, leaving some space at either end. Cook under a preheated hot broiler, in batches, for about 2 minutes, turning once. You cannot see if the chicken is cooked through, so test one piece, broiling it for a little longer if necessary. Keep the cooked chicken warm while you cook the remaining skewers.

garnish the skewers with chopped onion and cucumber chunks and serve with the satay sauce.

Serves 4
Preparation time: *20 minutes, plus marinating*
Cooking time: *about 15 minutes*

Shrimp and Corn Fritters

Many types of dipping sauce accompany Thai meals. Offer them in separate small bowls so that diners can experiment with the different flavors.

3 tablespoons self-rising flour

2½ oz raw peeled shrimp, finely chopped

I teaspoon Red Curry Paste (see page 12)

¼ cup canned, drained corn kernels

I egg white

I kaffir lime leaf, shredded

oil, for deep-frying

cilantro sprigs, to garnish (optional)

Hot Sweet Sauce (see page 246), to serve

Soy and vinegar dipping sauce

3 tablespoons distilled white vinegar or Chinese rice vinegar

3 tablespoons dark soy sauce

1½ teaspoons superfine sugar

2 small fresh chilies, finely sliced

make the dipping sauce. Mix all the sauce ingredients together in a bowl and stir until the sugar dissolves. Set aside.

mix together the flour, shrimp, curry paste, corn kernels, egg white, and lime leaf in a separate bowl.

heat the oil in a wok or deep skillet to 350–375°F, or until a cube of bread browns in 30 seconds. Drop 1 heaping tablespoon of the fritter mixture at a time into the hot oil, in 2 batches if necessary, and deep-fry for about 5 minutes, or until golden brown. Remove with a slotted spoon and drain on paper towels. Transfer to a serving dish.

garnish with cilantro sprigs, if desired, and serve with the dipping sauce and the hot sweet sauce.

Serves 4
Preparation time: *10 minutes*
Cooking time: *5–10 minutes*

Steamed Won Ton

Won ton skins are widely available in Asian markets, but if you cannot find them, you could use egg roll skins or phyllo pastry instead. Cut the sheets to size and cover them with a damp dishtowel while you work.

16 won ton skins

oil, for drizzling

Filling

6 raw shrimp, peeled

4 oz ground pork

3 tablespoons finely chopped onion

2 garlic cloves, finely chopped

5 canned, drained water chestnuts, finely chopped

1 teaspoon palm sugar or light brown sugar

1 tablespoon soy sauce

1 egg

To serve

Soy and Vinegar Dipping Sauce (see page 26)

Hot Sweet Sauce (see page 246)

make the filling. Mix all the filling ingredients together in a bowl to form a thick paste.

put 1 heaping teaspoonful of the filling in the center of a won ton skin, placed over your thumb and index finger. As you push the filled skin down through the circle that your fingers form, tighten the top, shaping it but leaving the top open. Repeat with the remaining skins.

put the filled won tons on a plate and place the plate in a steamer. Drizzle a little oil on top of the won tons, cover, and steam for 30 minutes.

serve the won tons either hot or warm with the dipping sauce and the hot sweet sauce.

Makes 16
Preparation time: *15 minutes*
Cooking time: *30 minutes*

Toasted Chili Cashew Nuts

1⅓ cups unroasted, unsalted cashew nuts

1 tablespoon peanut oil

1 garlic clove, finely chopped

¼ teaspoon crushed dried chilies

1 scallion, finely chopped

2 small fresh chilies (different colors), finely chopped

salt

dry-fry the cashew nuts in a wok or skillet, using no oil, stirring constantly until golden brown. Remove from the heat and allow to cool.

heat the oil in a wok or large skillet over a moderate heat and stir-fry the garlic for 1 minute, or until golden. Remove with a slotted spoon and set aside.

add the nuts to the oil and sprinkle with the crushed dried chilies. Stir-fry for 1 minute, then add the scallion, chopped fresh chilies, garlic, and salt to taste and stir-fry briefly. Serve warm.

Serves 4
Preparation time: *5 minutes*
Cooking time: *5 minutes*

clipboard: Chilies are an essential element in Thai cooking. Dried chilies are hotter than fresh ones, and just 1 or 2 small dried red chilies or a small quantity of crushed dried chilies or chili flakes will add a significant amount of heat.

Raw Vegetables with Yellow Bean Sauce

about 1 lb mixed raw vegetables of your choice, such as carrots, red and orange bell peppers, and cucumber

to garnish

1 fresh red chili, sliced into rings

flowering chives (optional)

Yellow bean sauce

6 tablespoons yellow bean sauce

½ onion, chopped

1 tablespoon tamarind water (see right)

¾ cup coconut milk

¾ cup water

2 eggs

3 tablespoons palm sugar or light brown sugar

1 tablespoon soy sauce

cut all the vegetables into bite-size pieces.

make the sauce. Put the yellow bean sauce and onion in a food processor and process until blended. Turn into a saucepan. Add the remaining sauce ingredients and bring slowly to a boil over a low heat, stirring. Remove from the heat and pour the sauce into a serving bowl.

garnish the sauce with the sliced red chili and serve warm with the prepared vegetables, garnished with flowering chives, if desired.

Serves 4
Preparation time: *15 minutes*
Cooking time: *5–6 minutes*

clipboard: Tamarind has a distinctive, rather sour flavor. It is obtained from the seed pods of a tree that originated in Africa but that was widely planted in India before being cultivated commercially. The pulp from the pods is used in Thai cooking. Simmer dried pulp for 2–3 minutes, cool, then squeeze out the juice (discarding the pulp and seeds). Alternatively, dissolve a spoonful of concentrate in hot water.

Stuffed Green Bell Peppers

8 large green bell peppers

about 3 cups peanut oil, for deep-frying

chives, to garnish

Filling

3 baby corn, roughly chopped

3 garlic cloves, halved

4 tablespoons peanut oil

½ large onion, finely chopped

1 tomato, diced

2 fresh shiitake mushrooms, finely sliced

½ cup green beans, finely sliced

½ teaspoon palm sugar or light brown sugar

1 tablespoon soy sauce

¼ teaspoon salt

1 teaspoon pepper

2 eggs

Batter

3 tablespoons cornstarch

3 tablespoons water

½ teaspoon salt

¼ teaspoon pepper

cut the tops off the peppers, remove the cores and seeds and set the hollow peppers aside.

make the filling. Put the baby corn and garlic in a food processor and process until blended.

heat 3 tablespoons of the oil in a wok or large skillet over a moderately high heat and stir-fry the onion for 30 seconds. Add the tomato and mushrooms and stir-fry for 1 minute. Add the green beans and stir-fry for 30 seconds then add the corn and garlic mixture, the sugar, soy sauce, salt, and pepper. At this point you may need to add the remaining oil.

break the eggs into the mixture and stir well. Cook for 2 minutes, then remove the pan from the heat and turn the mixture onto a plate. Stuff the peppers with the filling, making sure that they are as full as possible.

make the batter. Beat all the batter ingredients together in a bowl. Heat the oil in a wok or deep skillet to 350–375°F, or until a cube of bread browns in 30 seconds. Coat half the peppers in the batter, drop them into the hot oil and deep-fry, moving them around gently, for 6–7 minutes until golden brown on all sides. Remove with a slotted spoon and drain on paper towels. Repeat with the remaining peppers and batter.

arrange the cooked peppers on a serving plate, garnish with chives, and serve immediately.

Makes 8
Preparation time: *25 minutes*
Cooking time: *12–14 minutes*

Thai Egg Strips

Omelets are popular snacks in Thailand, widely available in markets and from roadside vendors. This is a quick and easy dish, but looks impressive.

3 eggs, beaten

1 shallot, finely sliced

green shoots of 1 scallion, sliced

1–2 small fresh red chilies, finely chopped

1 tablespoon chopped cilantro leaves

1 tablespoon peanut oil

salt and pepper

very fine strips of scallion, to garnish (optional)

mix together all the ingredients, except the oil, in a bowl.

heat the oil in a wok or large skillet over a moderately high heat, pour in the egg mixture and swirl it around the pan to form a large, thin omelet. Cook for 1–2 minutes until firm.

slide the omelet out onto a plate and roll it up as though it were a crepe. Allow to cool.

when the omelet is cool, cut the roll crosswise into ¼ inch or ½ inch sections, depending on how wide you want your strips to be. Serve them, still rolled up or straightened out, in a heap, garnished with very fine strips of scallion, if desired.

Serves 4
Preparation time: *5 minutes*
Cooking time: *2–3 minutes*

Son-in-law Eggs

Palm sugar, derived from the coconut palm and available in blocks or cans, is widely used in Southeast Asian cooking. Use light brown sugar if you cannot find palm sugar.

4 hard-cooked eggs

about 3 cups peanut oil, for deep-frying

5 shallots, finely sliced

3 large garlic cloves, finely sliced

⅓ cup tamarind water (see page 32)

3 tablespoons vegetarian nam pla (fish sauce) or 1 teaspoon salt

⅓ cup palm sugar or light brown sugar

½ cup water

To garnish

2 large fresh red chilies, seeded and diagonally sliced

cilantro leaves

shell the eggs and cut them in half lengthwise.

heat the oil in a wok or large skillet over a moderate heat and stir-fry the shallots and garlic until golden. Remove with a slotted spoon, drain on paper towels and set aside.

slide the eggs, yolk side down, into the hot oil. Cook until golden all over. Remove with a slotted spoon, drain on paper towels and set aside.

put the tamarind water, nam pla or salt, and sugar in a saucepan. Stir until the sugar dissolves, then add the measurement water. Cook, stirring constantly, for 5 minutes, or until the sauce becomes syrupy. Reduce the heat.

arrange the eggs, yolk side up, on a plate and sprinkle with the shallots and garlic. Bring the sauce to a fast boil and continue boiling until it is reduced and thickened. Remove from the heat and ladle over the eggs.

serve hot, garnished with the sliced red chilies and cilantro leaves.

Serves 4
Preparation time: *20 minutes*
Cooking time: *15 minutes*

Egg Rolls

Nam pla, a fish sauce that is used in numerous Thai dishes, is made from salted, fermented fish. It has a strong flavor and a very distinctive smell.

8 oz egg roll skins, each about 5 inches square

1 egg, beaten

oil, for deep-frying

Filling

2 tablespoons vegetable oil

2 tablespoons Garlic Mixture (see page 250)

4 oz crabmeat

4 oz raw shrimp, peeled and finely chopped

4 oz ground pork

4 oz dried rice vermicelli, soaked in hot water for 15–20 minutes, drained, and cut into ½ inch lengths

1¼ cups chopped mushrooms

2 tablespoons nam pla (fish sauce)

2 tablespoons soy sauce

1 teaspoon palm sugar or light brown sugar

5 scallions, finely chopped

To garnish

1 large fresh red chili, cut into fine strips

1 lime, sliced

basil sprigs

make the filling. Heat the oil in a wok or large skillet over a moderate heat and stir-fry the garlic mixture for 1 minute until golden. Add the crabmeat, shrimp, and pork and stir-fry for 10–12 minutes, or until lightly cooked. Add the vermicelli, mushrooms, nam pla, soy sauce, sugar, and scallions and stir-fry for an additional 5 minutes, or until all the liquid has been absorbed. Allow to cool.

separate the egg roll skins and spread them out under a damp dishtowel to keep them soft. Put about 2 tablespoons of the filling on each skin and brush the left and right borders with beaten egg.

fold the sides over the filling and roll it up like a sausage. Brush the top edge with more beaten egg and seal. Keep the filled rolls covered while you make the remaining rolls in the same way.

heat the oil in a wok or deep skillet to 350–375°F, or until a cube of bread browns in 30 seconds. Deep-fry the egg rolls, a few at a time, for 5–8 minutes, or until golden brown. Turn them once during cooking so that they brown evenly. Remove with a slotted spoon and drain on paper towels. Serve hot, garnished with fine strips of red chili, lime slices, and basil sprigs.

Serves 6
Preparation time: *25 minutes*
Cooking time: *30–40 minutes*

Fried Won Ton

8 oz ground pork

1 tablespoon finely chopped onion

2 teaspoons Garlic Mixture (see page 250)

½ tablespoon nam pla (fish sauce)

20 won ton skins (suitable for frying), each about 5 inches square

1 egg yolk, beaten

oil, for deep-frying

Plum Sauce (see page 46) or Chili Sauce (see page 138), to serve

1 scallion, cut into very fine strips, to garnish

mix together the pork, onion, garlic mixture, and nam pla in a bowl to form a thick paste.

spread out the won ton skins on a work surface and put a teaspoon of the pork mixture in the center of each skin.

brush the edges of the skins with egg yolk and pull the 4 corners up into the center to make little bags.

heat the oil in a wok or deep skillet to 350–375°F, or until a cube of bread browns in 30 seconds. Deep-fry the won ton, a few at a time, for about 5 minutes, or until golden brown. Turn them over in the oil if necessary to brown both sides. Remove with a slotted spoon and drain on paper towels.

serve the won tons hot with plum sauce or chili sauce, garnished with very fine strips of scallion.

Serves 4–5
Preparation time: *15 minutes*
Cooking time: *20 minutes*

Fried Golden Bags

If necessary, you can make the little pouches up to about three hours in advance, keeping them covered in the refrigerator. You can also freeze the filled, uncooked pouches.

20 won ton skins (suitable for frying), each about 5 inches square

20 flowering chives, about 4 inches long, plus extra to garnish

oil, for deep-frying

Plum Sauce (see page 46) or Chili Sauce (see page 138), to serve

Filling

½ cup canned, drained, chopped water chestnuts

8 oz crabmeat

2 oz raw shrimp, peeled and finely chopped

2 teaspoons Garlic Mixture (see page 250)

2 scallions, chopped

1 fresh green chili, seeded and chopped

1 tablespoon dark soy sauce

1 tablespoon nam pla (fish sauce)

make the filling. Mix all the filling ingredients together in a large bowl to form a thick paste.

spread out the won ton skins on a work surface and divide the crabmeat filling equally between them, putting a spoonful in the center of each skin. Pull the 4 corners up into the center to make little bags.

use the chives to secure the little bags around the center where the corners of the wrappers are gathered together. Take care that the chives do not break as you tie them.

heat the oil in a wok or deep skillet to 350–375°F, or until a cube of bread browns in 30 seconds. Deep-fry the little bags, a few at a time, for 2–3 minutes until crisp and golden brown. Remove with a slotted spoon and drain on paper towels.

serve very hot with plum sauce or chili sauce, garnished with a few extra flowering chives.

Serves 4–5
Preparation time: *25 minutes*
Cooking time: *8–12 minutes*

Thai Shrimp toasts

Mooli comes from the same vegetable family as the radish, which can be used instead, but it is much larger and has a slightly less peppery taste.

3 oz raw shrimp, peeled and finely chopped

4 oz ground pork

1 tablespoon cilantro leaves, finely chopped, plus extra to garnish

1 tablespoon finely chopped scallion

1 teaspoon Garlic Mixture (see page 250)

1 tablespoon nam pla (fish sauce)

1 egg, beaten

5 slices white bread

5 tablespoons sesame seeds

oil, for deep-frying

Plum sauce

5 tablespoons distilled white vinegar or Chinese rice vinegar

4 tablespoons plum jelly

1 small fresh red chili, finely sliced

To serve

¼ green bell pepper, thinly sliced

ribbons of raw mooli

make the plum sauce. Put the vinegar and jelly in a small saucepan and heat gently, mixing thoroughly. Remove the pan from the heat, turn the sauce into a small serving bowl and allow to cool. Add the chili before serving.

put the shrimp and pork into a bowl with the cilantro, scallion, garlic mixture, and nam pla. Add the egg and mix well.

cut each slice of bread into 4 roughly equal pieces and spread each one with some of the shrimp and pork mixture, using a knife to press the mixture firmly onto the bread. Sprinkle with the sesame seeds.

heat about 1 inch of oil in a wok or deep skillet to 350–375°F, or until a cube of bread browns in 30 seconds. Deep-fry the pieces of bread, a few at a time, topping side down, for 6–8 minutes, then turn them over and cook the other side until golden brown. Remove with a slotted spoon and drain on paper towels.

garnish with chopped cilantro and serve hot with the plum sauce, thin slices of green bell pepper, and ribbons of mooli.

Serves 4
Preparation time: *15 minutes*
Cooking time: *8–10 minutes*

Deep-fried Corn Cakes

Soy sauce, made from fermented soybeans, is an essential ingredient in almost all Asian cuisines, and it is available in all supermarkets and large food stores.

1 lb corn ears

1 lb ground pork (not too lean)

1 tablespoon Garlic Mixture (see page 250)

2 eggs, beaten

2 tablespoons all-purpose flour

1 tablespoon cornstarch

1 teaspoon salt

2 tablespoons soy sauce

½ vegetable bouillon cube, crumbled (optional)

oil, for deep-frying

2 tablespoons cilantro leaves, chopped, to garnish

To serve

1 large cucumber, very thinly sliced

12 fresh red chilies, seeded and cut into very fine strips

working over a bowl, slice the kernels off the corn ears with a sharp knife. Add the pork and garlic mixture and mix well, then stir in half the beaten egg.

add the flour, cornstarch, salt, and soy sauce, stirring well to make a mixture that is firm enough to be shaped. Add more beaten egg if necessary. Break off a small piece of the mixture and test-fry it in a little oil. If it tastes bland, mix in the crumbled bouillon cube.

form the mixture into flat, round cakes, each about 1½ inches across. Heat the oil in a wok or deep skillet to 350–375°F, or until a cube of bread browns in 30 seconds Deep-fry the cakes, a few at a time, until cooked and golden brown. Remove with a slotted spoon and drain on paper towels. Allow to cool.

arrange the corn cakes on a serving plate and garnish with chopped cilantro. Serve with cucumber slices and very fine strips of red chili.

Serves 4
Preparation time: *15 minutes*
Cooking time: *20 minutes*

Griddled Shrimp Cakes

Do not use instant mashed potato for this dish or the cakes will disintegrate when you fry them.

1 lb cooked peeled shrimp

1 garlic clove, crushed

1 inch piece of fresh gingerroot, peeled and diced

2 fresh red chilies, chopped

1 bunch of cilantro, chopped

2 teaspoons nam pla (fish sauce)

1 egg yolk

1 cup mashed potatoes

all-purpose flour, for dusting (optional)

soy sauce or Chili Sauce (see page 138), to serve

put the shrimp in a food processor with the garlic, ginger, chilies, cilantro, nam pla, and egg yolk and process until smooth.

transfer the shrimp mixture to a bowl, add the mashed potatoes and use a fork to mix together thoroughly. Form the mixture into 12 cakes, or 24 smaller ones if you prefer, dusting your hands in flour if the mixture is sticky.

heat a griddle pan over a moderately high heat. Cook the shrimp cakes, in 2 batches, on the griddle for 5 minutes on each side. Keep the cooked cakes warm while you cook the remaining shrimp cakes.

serve hot with some soy or chili sauce.

Serves 4
Preparation time: *10 minutes*
Cooking time: *20 minutes*

Broiled Shrimp and Scallops with Pineapple

10 oz raw shrimp, peeled and deveined

10 oz raw scallops, shelled and cleaned

I fresh pineapple, cut into I inch cubes

marinade

2 garlic cloves, finely chopped

I tablespoon finely chopped cilantro leaves

I long fresh red chili, seeded and finely chopped

I tablespoon sesame oil

I½ tablespoons light soy sauce

½ teaspoon ground white pepper

make the marinade. Mix all the marinade ingredients together in a bowl. Add the shrimp and scallops and turn in the marinade to coat thoroughly. Cover and allow to marinate in the refrigerator for at least 30 minutes.

divide the shrimp and scallops into separate groups. Thread the shrimp and pineapple alternately onto 4 presoaked bamboo skewers (see below), leaving some space at either end. Thread the scallops and the remaining pineapple onto another 4 presoaked bamboo skewers.

cook the skewers under a preheated hot broiler for 8–10 minutes, turning once, until the shrimp and scallops are cooked through and tender. Serve hot.

Serves 4
Preparation time: *20 minutes, plus marinating*
Cooking time: *8–10 minutes*

clipboard: Use bamboo skewers 7–8 inches long and soak them in cold water for about 1 hour before you need them to help stop them burning during cooking.

Soups

Red Pork Noodle Soup

Chinese flowering cabbage, choy sum, is a member of the same family as bok choy. It has light green leaves, long stems, and yellow flowers, and can be eaten on its own as a steamed vegetable or added to soups and stir-fries.

6 oz fresh egg noodles

1 teaspoon Garlic Oil (see page 250)

2 choy sum, sliced

1½ teaspoons finely sliced scallion

1 tablespoon soy sauce

2 tablespoons cilantro leaves

pinch of pepper

8 oz Red Roast Pork, sliced (see page 122)

2½ cups Chicken Stock (see page 14)

Dipping sauce

4 tablespoons distilled white vinegar

2–3 tablespoons nam pla (fish sauce)

1 large fresh red chili, sliced

cook the noodles in a large saucepan of boiling water for 2–3 minutes, untangling them while they are boiling. Drain and mix in the garlic oil to prevent sticking.

meanwhile, cook the choy sum in a separate saucepan of boiling water for 1 minute, drain and reserve.

put the noodles in a large, heatproof serving bowl, then add the choy sum, scallion, soy sauce, cilantro leaves, and pepper. Arrange the pork slices on the top. Heat the stock to boiling point and pour it over the pork, noodles, and vegetables.

combine all the ingredients for the dipping sauce in a small bowl and serve with the soup.

Serves 4
Preparation time: *10 minutes*
Cooking time: *5 minutes*

Mussel Soup

Similar in appearance to glass (cellophane) noodles, rice vermicelli are used in salads and egg rolls as well as in soups, as here. They should always be soaked in hot water to soften them before use.

1 lb live mussels

1¼ cups coconut milk

2½ cups Fish Stock (see page 15)

3 oz dried rice vermicelli, soaked in hot water for 15–20 minutes and drained

1 tablespoon peeled and finely chopped fresh gingerroot

1 cup cilantro stalks and roots

½ lemon grass stalk, chopped

2 small fresh red chilies, finely sliced

1 tablespoon nam pla (fish sauce)

1 tablespoon lime juice

½ cup cilantro leaves, to garnish

wash the mussels in cold water and scrape away any barnacles with a sharp knife. Remove the beards, then leave the mussels to soak for about 1 hour in cold water. Drain and tap any open shells to make sure that they close. Discard any mussels that remain open.

put the mussels in a saucepan, cover and cook over a moderate heat, shaking the pan occasionally, for 3–4 minutes until they have opened. Discard any that remain closed. Remove the mussels with a slotted spoon and reserve.

add all the remaining ingredients to the pan and simmer for 15 minutes. Return the mussels to the pan and simmer for 1 minute. Serve hot, garnished with cilantro leaves.

Serves 4
Preparation time: *20 minutes, plus soaking*
Cooking time: *20 minutes*

Glass Noodle Soup

Glass or cellophane noodles are also known as bean thread noodles or bean vermicelli. Soak them for about 15 minutes in hot water to soften before use.

1/3 large cucumber, roughly chopped

1 onion, halved

2 garlic cloves, halved

2/3 cup chopped white cabbage

2 1/2 cups water

4 oz dried glass noodles, soaked for about 15 minutes in hot water and drained

1 oz dried tofu sheets, soaked for 2–3 hours, drained, and torn into pieces

1/2 oz dried lily flowers, soaked and drained, or canned, drained bamboo shoots, thinly sliced

1 teaspoon salt

1 teaspoon palm sugar or light brown sugar

1/2 teaspoon soy sauce

2 large dried shiitake mushrooms, soaked in warm water for 15–20 minutes, drained, and thinly sliced, hard stalks cut away and added to a stockpot

chopped celery leaves, to garnish

put the cucumber, onion, garlic, and cabbage in a food processor and process for 15 seconds. Turn the mixture into a saucepan and add the measurement water. Bring to a boil, then reduce the heat and cook for 2 minutes, stirring occasionally.

strain the stock into a larger saucepan and add the noodles, tofu, lily flowers or bamboo shoots, salt, sugar, and soy sauce. Stir well, then cook over a moderate heat for about 3 minutes. Taste and adjust the seasoning, if necessary.

pour the soup into a serving bowl, arrange the mushroom slices in the center and sprinkle with chopped celery leaves. Serve immediately.

Serves 4
Preparation time: *10 minutes, plus soaking*
Cooking time: *about 5 minutes*

Khun Tom's Pumpkin Soup

1 teaspoon finely sliced lemon grass

1 teaspoon peeled and finely sliced fresh galangal

1 tablespoon basil leaves

½ green bell pepper, cored, seeded, and chopped

3 kaffir lime leaves

½ cup water

1 tablespoon peanut oil

2 garlic cloves, finely chopped

10 shallots, thinly sliced

1 teaspoon crushed dried chilies

1 small fresh red chili, chopped

2 cups Vegetable Stock (see page 15)

½ cup green beans, chopped

3 tablespoons vegetarian nam pla (fish sauce) or soy sauce

3 cups cubed pumpkin

1 teaspoon palm sugar or light brown sugar

1 teaspoon ground white pepper

1 tablespoon Crushed Roasted Nuts (see page 248) or crunchy peanut butter

3 teaspoons curry powder

¾ cup coconut milk

2 teaspoons cornstarch

Crispy Basil (see page 248), to garnish

put the lemon grass, galangal, basil leaves, bell pepper, lime leaves, and measurement water in a food processor and process until blended, then strain and discard the water, reserving the puree.

heat the oil in a wok or large skillet. Add the garlic, shallots, and crushed dried and fresh chilies and stir-fry over a high heat for 1 minute.

add the puree, 1¾ cups of the stock, the green beans, nam pla or soy sauce, and pumpkin and stir over a moderate heat. Add the sugar, pepper, nuts or peanut butter, and curry powder and stir again. Cook, stirring frequently, for 10 minutes, or until the pumpkin is tender, then add the coconut milk, bring to a boil and boil hard for 1 minute.

blend the remaining stock with the cornstarch to form a smooth paste, add to the soup and cook, stirring, until thickened.

ladle the soup into a large serving bowl, top with the crispy basil and serve immediately.

Serves 4
Preparation time: *30 minutes*
Cooking time: *15 minutes*

Banana Soup

The bananas used by Thai cooks tend to be smaller and sweeter than the ones normally found in Western supermarkets, but this savory soup uses a single large banana.

1 tablespoon peanut oil

3 tablespoons sliced scallions (including green shoots)

1½ tablespoons sliced garlic

¾ cup coconut milk

1¾ cups Vegetable Stock (see page 15)

¼ teaspoon ground white pepper

3 teaspoons vegetarian nam pla (fish sauce) or soy sauce

¼ teaspoon salt

½ teaspoon palm sugar or light brown sugar

1 large banana, peeled and diagonally cut into thin slices

1 large fresh red chili, diagonally sliced

very fine strips of scallion, to garnish

heat the oil in a wok or large skillet over a moderately high heat and stir-fry the scallions and garlic for 1–2 minutes. Add all the other ingredients and cook, stirring frequently, for 5 minutes.

if you prefer a blended soup, set aside about one-quarter of the banana and chili slices, then puree the remainder with the soup in a food processor or blender until smooth. Return the blended mixture to the pan, add the reserved banana and chili slices and warm through for 3 minutes.

serve immediately, garnished with very fine strips of scallion.

Serves 4
Preparation time: *15 minutes*
Cooking time: *10 minutes*

Chicken and Coconut Milk Soup

2½ cups Chicken Stock (see page 14)

6 kaffir lime leaves, torn, or ¼ teaspoon grated lime zest

1 lemon grass stalk, diagonally sliced, or ¼ teaspoon grated lemon zest

2 inch piece of fresh galangal or gingerroot, peeled and finely sliced

¾ cup coconut milk

½ cup nam pla (fish sauce)

2 teaspoons palm sugar or light brown sugar

6 tablespoons lime juice

8 oz boneless chicken, skinned and cut into small pieces

4 tablespoons chili oil or 4 small fresh red chilies, finely sliced into rings (optional)

heat the stock in a saucepan over a moderate heat, then stir in the lime leaves or lime zest, lemon grass or lemon zest, and galangal or ginger. As the stock is simmering, add the coconut milk, nam pla, sugar, and lime juice. Stir well, then add the chicken and simmer for 5 minutes.

just before serving, add the chili oil or chilies, if desired, stir again and serve immediately.

Serves 4
Preparation time: *6 minutes*
Cooking time: *10 minutes*

clipboard: To make coconut cream and milk, mix together 4 cups grated fresh coconut or shredded coconut and 3½ cups milk in a saucepan. Bring to a boil, then reduce the heat and simmer, stirring occasionally, until the mixture is reduced by one-third. Strain, pressing the mixture against the side of the strainer to extract as much liquid as possible. Pour the strained coconut milk into a bowl and chill in the refrigerator. When it is really cold, skim off the thicker "cream" that rises to the surface. The remaining liquid is the coconut milk.

Shrimp and Lime Soup

The roots of cilantro are used in many Thai dishes, but only the refreshing leaves are added to this delicious soup, which can be served with rice.

1½ lb raw shrimp

8 cups water

6 small kaffir lime leaves or ¼ teaspoon grated lime zest

1 tablespoon chopped lemon grass or ¼ teaspoon grated lemon zest

2 teaspoons nam pla (fish sauce)

5 tablespoons lime juice

4 tablespoons cilantro leaves, chopped

3 tablespoons sliced scallions

1 fresh red chili, seeded and sliced into 1 inch strips

salt and pepper (optional)

very fine strips of scallion, to garnish

peel the shrimp and remove the dark vein running along the back. Rinse under cold running water and pat dry with paper towels. Set aside while you make the soup.

pour the measurement water into a large saucepan and bring to a boil. Add the lime leaves or lime zest and lemon grass or lemon zest, reduce the heat and simmer for 10 minutes. Add the nam pla and cook for an additional 5 minutes.

add the shrimp and lime juice to the pan and cook over a low heat for a few minutes until the shrimp have turned pink and are cooked through.

add the cilantro, scallions, and chili to the soup. Taste and adjust the seasoning, if necessary, and serve very hot in individual bowls, garnished with very fine strips of scallion.

Serves 6
Preparation time: *15 minutes*
Cooking time: *20 minutes*

Rice Noodle Soup

Tofu is a white curd, derived from unfermented soybean paste, and sometimes known as beancurd. You can buy pieces of soft tofu that have been deep-fried so that the outside has a brown crust and the center is hard and dry.

3 cups Vegetable Stock (see page 15)

3 scallions, cut into 1 inch lengths

2 baby corn, diagonally sliced

1 tomato, finely diced

1 red onion, cut into slivers

6 kaffir lime leaves or ¼ teaspoon grated lime zest

1 celery stick, chopped

4 oz ready-fried tofu, diced

1 tablespoon soy sauce

1 teaspoon pepper

1 heaping teaspoon crushed dried chilies

6 oz dried wide rice noodles, soaked for about 15 minutes in hot water and drained

cilantro sprigs, to garnish

lime quarters, to serve (optional)

heat the stock in a saucepan over a moderate heat, then add all the remaining ingredients, except the noodles and a few of the red onion slivers, and stir well.

bring to a boil and boil for 30 seconds, then reduce the heat and simmer for 5 minutes. Add the noodles and simmer for a further 2 minutes.

pour into a serving bowl, garnish with cilantro sprigs and the remaining red onion slivers, and serve with lime quarters, if desired.

Serves 4
Preparation time: *10 minutes, plus soaking*
Cooking time: *10 minutes*

Clear Tofu Soup

Tofu is ideal for use in soups because it takes on the other flavors of the dish. This is a quick and easy soup to make.

4 cups Vegetable Stock (see page 15)

8 oz ground pork

10 oz firm tofu, cut into large squares

2 cups fresh bean sprouts

4 tablespoons nam pla (fish sauce)

2 scallions, finely chopped

1 celery stick with leaves, chopped

pepper

heat the stock in a saucepan over a moderate heat. Put the pork in a bowl, add about 1 cup of the hot stock and stir with a fork to break up the meat so that no lumps remain.

add the pork mixture to the stock in the pan and cook over a moderate heat for 5 minutes. Stir in the tofu, bean sprouts, nam pla, scallions, and celery and bring to a boil. Reduce the heat and simmer for a further 3 minutes.

transfer the soup to a serving bowl, season with pepper and serve on its own as a starter or as an accompaniment to the main meal, in the traditional Thai way.

Serves 4
Preparation time: *10 minutes*
Cooking time: *10 minutes*

clipboard: You can store fresh tofu in the refrigerator for up to 4 days. Cover it with water and make sure that you change the water every day.

Salads

Ground Fish Salad

Catfish is a notoriously bony fish, and you might find that you need to use tweezers to pick out all the little bones.

1¼ lb whole catfish, cleaned

12 small fresh green chilies, finely sliced

½ red onion, finely sliced

¼ cup cilantro leaves, stalks, and roots, finely chopped, plus extra leaves to garnish

3 tablespoons lime juice

3 tablespoons nam pla (fish sauce)

1½ tablespoons palm sugar or light brown sugar

¼ large, hard green mango, peeled and grated (optional)

⅓ cup Crushed Roasted Nuts (see page 248)

about 3 cups oil, for deep-frying

To garnish
shredded white cabbage

whole fresh red chilies

put the catfish in a foil-lined broiler pan and cook under a preheated moderate broiler for 30 minutes or until cooked and tender, turning the fish over halfway through the cooking time. Allow to cool.

skin the fish and remove the flesh, carefully discarding any bones. Grind the fish in a food processor or chop it very finely and set aside.

put all the remaining ingredients, except the oil, in a bowl and mix well to make a sauce.

heat the oil in a wok or deep skillet to 350–375°F, or until a cube of bread browns in 30 seconds. Deep-fry the ground fish, in batches, for 4–5 minutes, stirring occasionally. Remove with a slotted spoon and drain on paper towels.

arrange the ground fish on a serving dish. Pour the sauce over the top of the fish and serve, garnished with shredded cabbage, cilantro leaves, and whole red chilies.

Serves 4
Preparation time: *15 minutes*
Cooking time: *45 minutes*

Deep-fried Dried Fish Salad

Mangoes can have green, yellow, red, or purple flesh, but the green mangoes used here have a much tarter flavor than the larger, yellow-fleshed fruits used in desserts.

6 small fresh green and red chilies, finely sliced

½ red onion, finely chopped

½ cup cilantro leaves, stalks, and roots, finely chopped, plus extra leaves to garnish

2 tablespoons lime juice

½ tablespoon nam pla (fish sauce)

1½ tablespoons palm sugar or light brown sugar

¼ large, hard green mango, peeled and grated, plus extra matchsticks to garnish

about 3 cups oil, for deep-frying

2 oz small dried fish

lettuce leaves, to serve

put the chilies and red onion in a mortar and pound with a pestle to a thick paste. Add the chopped cilantro and pound again. Add the lime juice, nam pla, sugar, and green mango and pound once more until the ingredients are thoroughly blended.

heat the oil in a wok or large skillet to 350–375°F, or until a cube of bread browns in 30 seconds. Deep-fry the dried fish, in batches, for 2–3 minutes until golden and crisp. Remove with a slotted spoon and drain on paper towels.

arrange some lettuce leaves on a serving dish and place the fish on top. Pour over the sauce from the mortar, garnish with cilantro leaves and serve immediately.

Serves 4
Preparation time: *10–15 minutes*
Cooking time: *5 minutes*

Glass Noodle Salad

Glass or cellophane noodles are often sold dried in bundles.

Do not oversoak or they will disintegrate when cooked.

8 oz dried glass noodles, soaked for about 15 minutes in hot water and drained

1 tomato, halved and sliced

1 celery stick, chopped

1 scallion, chopped

1 onion, halved and sliced

½ green bell pepper, cored, seeded, and chopped

juice of 2 limes

5 small fresh green chilies, finely chopped

2 teaspoons palm sugar or light brown sugar

½ cup Crushed Roasted Nuts—use peanuts (see page 248)

1 teaspoon crushed dried chilies

½ teaspoon salt

2½ tablespoons vegetarian nam pla (fish sauce) or soy sauce

cilantro sprigs, to garnish

cook the noodles in a saucepan of boiling water for 3–4 minutes. Drain and rinse under cold running water to prevent further cooking.

cut the noodles into pieces about 5 inches long. Put them in a large serving bowl, add all the remaining ingredients, and mix thoroughly for 2 minutes.

serve the salad at room temperature, garnished with cilantro sprigs.

Serves 4
Preparation time: *15 minutes, plus soaking*
Cooking time: *3–5 minutes*

Cucumber Salad with Roasted Cashews

Thai cooks peel a cucumber by holding it flat and chopping it lengthways with a large knife and a quick motion, turning the cucumber as they go. They scrape off the long strips, then continue until they reach the seeds, which they discard.

1 cucumber

2 teaspoons palm sugar or light brown sugar

1½ teaspoons vegetarian nam pla (fish sauce) or soy sauce

1 cup Crushed Roasted Nuts—use cashew nuts (see page 248)

1 teaspoon crushed dried chilies

juice of 2 limes

½ teaspoon salt

peel the cucumber and chop it into long strips, discarding the seeds.

put the cucumber in a large serving bowl, add all the remaining ingredients, and toss together until thoroughly mixed.

serve the salad at room temperature.

Serves 4
Preparation time: *10 minutes*

Pomelo Salad

This refreshing salad could not be easier to make. If you cannot find pomelos, use grapefruit, which they closely resemble.

½ pomelo or 1 grapefruit

4 shallots, sliced

½ teaspoon crushed dried chilies

2 tablespoons palm sugar or light brown sugar

2 tablespoons vegetarian nam pla (fish sauce) or soy sauce

juice of 2 limes

¼ teaspoon salt

holding the fruit over a bowl, remove the membranes and separate and halve the segments. Discard the skin.

add all the remaining ingredients to the bowl and mix thoroughly. Serve the salad at room temperature.

Serves 4
Preparation time: *5 minutes*

clipboard: Pomelos, which are sometimes known as pummelos or shaddocks, are the largest of the citrus fruits, at about 12 inches across. They are widely used in Southeast Asia and are one of the antecedents of the grapefruit, although they are sweeter than that fruit.

Green Bean Salad

Use peanuts rather than cashew nuts in this recipe for an authentic combination. Treat the soft tofu carefully because it will quickly lose its shape when it is handled.

½ cup green beans, thinly sliced

½ cup silken tofu

½ cup coconut milk

I shallot, sliced

¼ cup Crushed Roasted Nuts—use peanuts (see page 248)

I teaspoon crushed dried chilies

I tablespoon lime juice

I teaspoon palm sugar or light brown sugar

2 tablespoons soy sauce

I teaspoon salt

cook the beans in a saucepan of boiling water for 2 minutes. Drain and set aside.

soften the tofu in the coconut milk in a saucepan over a low heat until it has partially melted. Remove the pan from the heat and add the beans and all the remaining ingredients.

stir the ingredients thoroughly to combine, then turn them out onto a serving dish. Serve the salad at room temperature.

Serves 6
Preparation time: *10 minutes*
Cooking time: *5–6 minutes*

Curried Vegetable Salad

2 celery sticks, roughly chopped

4 carrots, thinly sliced

1½ cups finely sliced cabbage

1 cup thin green beans

½ red bell pepper, cored, seeded, and diced

½ green bell pepper, cored, seeded, and diced

4 cups fresh bean sprouts

1¼ cups canned, drained, sliced water chestnuts

Curry dressing

4 oz creamed coconut

⅔ cup water

2 tablespoons peanut oil

2 tablespoons Red Curry Paste (see page 12)

2 tablespoons dark soy sauce

2 tablespoons lime juice

2 teaspoons palm sugar or light brown sugar

¼ teaspoon salt

1 teaspoon ground coriander

2 teaspoons ground cumin

3 tablespoons Crushed Roasted Nuts
(see page 248)

To garnish

slivers of fresh coconut

mint sprigs (optional)

cook all the vegetables, except the bean sprouts and water chestnuts, in a large saucepan of boiling water for 3–4 minutes. They should retain their fresh color and be slightly tender but still crisp. Drain and mix in a bowl with the bean sprouts and water chestnuts.

make the curry dressing. Put the creamed coconut in a separate bowl and cover with the measurement water. Stir well until the creamed coconut has completely dissolved, then set aside.

heat the oil in a wok or skillet over a low heat and stir-fry the curry paste for 1–2 minutes. Add the creamed coconut, soy sauce, lime juice, sugar, salt, coriander, cumin, and nuts. Stir well and heat through gently for 3–4 minutes. Pour the dressing over the vegetables and toss gently.

transfer the vegetables to a serving dish and serve warm, garnished with slivers of coconut, and mint sprigs, if desired.

Serves 4–6
Preparation time: *25 minutes*
Cooking time: *7–10 minutes*

Chicken and Papaya Salad

Papaya is often cooked and served with poultry or meat in Thailand as a cooling contrast to a spicy dressing. If papayas are difficult to obtain, use mango, pineapple, or melon instead.

Dressing

2 small fresh green or red chilies, seeded and chopped

2 large garlic cloves, chopped

finely grated zest of 1 lime

6 tablespoons lime juice

2–3 tablespoons nam pla (fish sauce)

2–3 tablespoons palm sugar or light brown sugar, to taste

Salad

1 lb chicken breast fillets, skinned

corn or peanut oil, for brushing

2 ripe papayas

1 crisp lettuce, such as iceberg, leaves separated

½ large cucumber, thinly sliced

1½ cups fresh bean sprouts

make the dressing. Put the chilies, garlic, and lime zest in a mortar and pound with a pestle to a paste.

stir in the lime juice and nam pla until evenly mixed with the chili and garlic paste, then add the sugar to taste. Cover and set aside while you prepare the salad ingredients and cook the chicken.

brush the chicken breasts liberally with oil. Cook under a preheated hot broiler for about 7 minutes on each side, or until cooked through.

peel the papayas and cut each one in half lengthwise. Scoop out and discard the seeds and slice the flesh thinly.

arrange the lettuce leaves around the edge of a serving dish, then place the papaya, cucumber, and bean sprouts attractively on top.

place the chicken on a cutting board. With a very sharp knife, cut it diagonally into bite-size slices. Arrange the chicken on top of the salad and sprinkle with the dressing. Allow the salad to stand for a few minutes before serving.

Serves 4
Preparation time: *30 minutes*
Cooking time: *15 minutes*

Sweet and Sour Salad

Remember to handle chilies with care. Wear gloves if your hands are sensitive, and be careful not to touch any part of your face, particularly your eyes, before you have washed your hands.

1 large garlic clove, chopped

2 fresh red bird's eye chilies, chopped

½ cup thinly sliced carrots

1½ cups thinly sliced white cabbage

2 green beans, cut into 1 inch lengths

2 tomatoes, chopped

1½ tablespoons nam pla (fish sauce)

3 tablespoons lemon juice

3 tablespoons palm sugar or light brown sugar

1 tablespoon ground dried shrimp

2 tablespoons Crushed Roasted Nuts (see page 248)

1 frisée lettuce, separated into leaves, to serve

basil sprigs, to garnish

put the garlic and chilies in a food processor and process to a thick paste. Alternatively, put them in a mortar and pound with a pestle.

transfer the mixture to a bowl, add the carrots, cabbage, green beans, tomatoes, nam pla, lemon juice, sugar, ground dried shrimp, and nuts and mix well so that all the ingredients are thoroughly blended.

arrange a bed of lettuce in a shallow serving dish, top with the salad, garnish with basil sprigs, and serve.

Serves 4
Preparation time: *15 minutes*

Green Mango Salad

Like papayas, mangoes are eaten ripe and unripe. The tart flavor of green mangoes can be bitter, and you might want to add a little more sugar to this refreshing salad.

1 large, hard green mango, peeled, seeded, and grated

1 red onion, chopped, plus extra slivers to garnish

2½ tablespoons palm sugar or light brown sugar

1 tablespoon lime juice

1 tablespoon soy sauce

½ teaspoon salt

1 teaspoon crushed dried chilies

½ cup Crushed Roasted Nuts (see page 248)

To garnish

cilantro leaves, finely chopped

1 fresh red chili, roughly chopped

stir together the mango and red onion in a large bowl. Add the sugar, lime juice, soy sauce, salt, and crushed dried chilies and stir thoroughly for 1–2 minutes.

add the nuts, give the salad a final stir and turn out onto a serving dish.

garnish the salad with chopped cilantro and red chili and slivers of red onion before serving.

Serves 3–4
Preparation time: *15 minutes*

Green Papaya Salad

Small bird's eye chilies have given Thai cooking its reputation for being hot. They are often used whole because cutting them up can make them even hotter.

12 oz green papayas, peeled and seeded

2 garlic cloves, crushed

3 fresh red bird's eye chilies, chopped, plus extra whole chilies to garnish

4 cherry tomatoes

2 tablespoons nam pla (fish sauce)

2 teaspoons superfine sugar

juice of 1 lime

1 tablespoon dried shrimp paste

3 tablespoons roasted peanuts, chopped

2 tablespoons roughly chopped cilantro leaves, plus extra leaves to garnish

roughly grate the papaya flesh or cut it into fine shreds.

put the garlic, chilies, and cherry tomatoes in a mortar and pound with a pestle to a rough puree.

add the grated papaya, nam pla, sugar, lime juice, and shrimp paste and pound together until roughly mixed.

add the chopped peanuts and cilantro and serve, garnished with the whole chilies and cilantro leaves.

Serves 4
Preparation time: *10 minutes*

clipboard: Some people are sensitive to the sap of green papayas, so wear disposable gloves the first time you handle this fruit. When it is grown in the tropics, the papaya tree bears fruit all year round, making it an important source of fruit.

Vegetables

Stir-fried Vegetables with Cashew Nuts

Make sure that all the vegetable pieces are more or less the same size so that they cook evenly and equally. Take care not to overcook them—the vegetables should have a definite "bite."

⅓ cup unroasted, unsalted cashew nuts

4 cups Chinese cabbage, chopped into 1 inch pieces

1 cup cauliflower florets

1 cup broccoli florets

⅔ cup chopped white cabbage

2 baby corn, diagonally sliced

1 tomato, cut into 8 pieces

5 garlic cloves, chopped

1½ tablespoons soy sauce

1 teaspoon palm sugar or light brown sugar

½ cup water

2½ tablespoons peanut oil

pepper (optional)

dry-fry the nuts in a skillet, using no oil, stirring constantly until golden brown. Remove from the heat and allow to cool.

put the nuts and all the remaining ingredients, except the oil and pepper, in a bowl and mix thoroughly.

heat the oil in a wok or large skillet over a high heat and stir-fry the contents of the bowl for 2–3 minutes. Taste and season with pepper, if necessary. Serve immediately.

Serves 3–4
Preparation time: *25 minutes*
Cooking time: *5–8 minutes*

Vegetables with Oyster Sauce

Vegetarians can use soy sauce in this recipe instead of oyster sauce, although it will not have the distinctive flavor of the fish-based sauce.

3 tablespoons vegetable oil

1 garlic clove, crushed

1½ cups shredded cabbage

2 cups cauliflower florets

½ teaspoon pepper

2 tablespoons oyster sauce

⅔ cup Chicken or Vegetable Stock (see pages 14–15)

2 cups broccoli florets

2 carrots, cut into fine strips, plus extra shredded carrot to garnish

1¼ cups thinly sliced mushrooms

1 onion, sliced into rings

1 cup fresh bean sprouts

boiled rice, to serve

heat the oil in a wok or large skillet over a moderate heat and stir-fry the garlic for 1 minute, or until golden. Do not allow it to get too brown.

add the cabbage, cauliflower, and pepper, then stir in the oyster sauce and stock. Cook, stirring constantly, for 3 minutes.

add the broccoli, carrots, mushrooms, onion, and bean sprouts and stir-fry for 2 minutes.

transfer the fried vegetables to a large warm dish or platter, garnish with shredded carrot and serve immediately with boiled rice.

Serves 4
Preparation time: *15 minutes*
Cooking time: *6–7 minutes*

Mushroom and Snow Pea Stir-fry

Shiitake mushrooms can be found dried in Asian markets, health food stores, and some supermarkets, which also sometimes sell them fresh.

10 dried shiitake mushrooms

1 tablespoon peanut oil

2 large garlic cloves, chopped

4 oz baby corn, diagonally sliced

1 cup drained, canned bamboo shoots

½ cup snow peas

1 teaspoon palm sugar or light brown sugar

3 tablespoons soy sauce

1 tablespoon water

pepper

to garnish

small green chilies

basil sprigs

soak the mushrooms in warm water for 15–20 minutes, then drain and slice. (The hard stalks should be cut away and added to a stockpot.)

heat the oil in a wok or large skillet over a high heat and briefly stir-fry the garlic, then add all the remaining ingredients, in turn, adding the mushrooms just before the bamboo shoots.

stir-fry the vegetables for 2–3 minutes, then turn out onto a serving dish. Garnish with green chilies and basil sprigs and serve immediately.

Serves 4
Preparation time: *10 minutes, plus soaking*
Cooking time: *3–4 minutes*

Stuffed Omelet

This is a popular lunchtime dish, often prepared and sold by roadside and market stalls.

about 1 tablespoon peanut oil

3 eggs, beaten

salt and pepper

Crispy Basil (see page 248), to garnish

Filling

3 tablespoons peanut oil

2 garlic cloves, chopped

1 onion, finely chopped

2 tablespoons chopped green beans

2 tablespoons chopped asparagus

3 baby corn, thinly sliced

1 tomato, diced

4 dried shiitake mushrooms, soaked for 15–20 minutes in warm water, drained and sliced, hard stalks cut away and added to a stockpot

1½ teaspoons palm sugar or light brown sugar

2 teaspoons soy sauce

3 tablespoons water

pinch of salt

make the filling. Heat the oil in a wok or skillet over a moderately high heat and stir-fry the garlic and onion for 30 seconds. Add the green beans, asparagus, baby corn, tomato, mushrooms, sugar, and soy sauce and stir-fry for 3–4 minutes. Add the measurement water and salt and stir-fry for a further 2 minutes. Remove the mixture from the pan and set aside. Wipe the pan clean with paper towels.

make the omelet. Heat the oil in the pan, making sure that it coats not only the base of the pan but as much of the side as possible. Pour off any excess. Pour in the eggs and swirl them around in the pan to form a large, thin omelet. Loosen the omelette and move it around with a spatula to make sure that it is not sticking to the pan, adding a little more oil if necessary.

when the omelet is almost firm, put the filling in the center and fold both sides and ends over to form an oblong parcel, constantly making sure that the omelet is not sticking underneath.

carefully remove the omelet from the pan and place it in a serving dish. Serve immediately, garnished with crispy basil.

Serves 1–2
Preparation time: *8–10 minutes, plus soaking*
Cooking time: *8–10 minutes*

Thai Dining

Thai people love snacking, and they often stop at market stalls several times a day to enjoy freshly cooked food. Meals eaten at home and in restaurants are taken in the same informal way. There are no distinct courses to a Thai meal, as there are in Western ones. Instead, a variety of dishes is presented at the same time, but each dish is carefully chosen in relation to the others, to provide a harmonious blend of flavors, textures, and cooking styles.

A Thai meal generally consists of a number of different dishes, plus a large bowl of rice. There might be a soup, served in a large bowl, which everyone can dip into, or in small individual bowls; a curry; something steamed or fried; a salad; some dipping sauces and pickles; and fresh fruit to finish the meal. All these dishes will appear on the table at the same time. Diners put a mound of rice on their plates, followed by a little of one of the other dishes. Thais do not put everything on their plates at once and eat it all together, as people do in the West. They like to appreciate all the different tastes and textures separately.

Thais use their fingers or a fork and spoon, unless they are eating noodles, when chopsticks, a sign of Chinese influence on Thai cuisine, are used.

You will not usually find a dessert on the menu, other than fruit, unless it is a special occasion. There are, however, a large number of Thai sweet dishes or sweetmeats, and a great many of them involve egg yolks and sugar, which is an indication of the Portuguese influence in this part of the world. Some take a long time to make and involve a number of different stages.

Menu planning

When you are planning a menu, keep the following points in mind and you will easily make some memorable meals.

Soups are popular dishes in Thailand. Often fiercely hot, they may be the only dish at a meal, especially in the middle of the day. However, it has become more usual for Thai restaurants, especially in the West, to serve a soup as the first course in a meal.

From traditional egg noodles to delicately flavored rice vermicelli, noodles often provide the basis of a Thai meal.

If you do not begin your meal with soup, a choice of two or three of the appetizers in this book will make an appealing light opening course for a Thai meal. Few Thais would object to this approach—after all, many of them buy their snacks two or three at a time from street vendors' stalls.

For the main part of the meal, choose dishes that work well together. A fiery meat or poultry curry could overpower a more delicate fish dish, for example. On the other hand, a fiery curry needs something cooling, like a simple rice dish or a fresh green salad, to complement and counteract the stronger flavors.

Do not serve dishes that have all been cooked in the same way—four stir-fries would all tend to have the same texture. Instead, plan for a variety of cooking styles, such as a stir-fry, a steamed dish, and, perhaps, something deep-fried. Similarly, try to vary the main ingredients, so that you have a meat dish, a fish dish, and a vegetable dish.

Thais, like most Asians, are not great dessert eaters. If you do not want to serve one of the desserts in this book, it is perfectly acceptable to serve a bowl of fresh fruits in season.

Rice and noodles

Rice and noodles provide the perfect accompaniment to more strongly flavored dishes. However, it is probably better to serve one or other of these at a meal, not both.

Thailand is not the largest rice producer in the world, but it is generally considered to produce the best quality rice, and the dual aspects of quality and quantity have led to it becoming the world's largest exporter of rice. Thai fragrant or jasmine rice is more expensive to buy than other long-grain rice, but it is so delicious that it is well worth paying extra for it, and Thai meals usually have a large bowl of hot jasmine rice at the center.

Creating a balance of different textures, colors, and fiery and cool or bland flavors is the key to a successful Thai meal.

Sticky or glutinous rice is often eaten with the fingers and formed into small balls, which are dipped into savory dishes, especially in the north of Thailand. It is also the basis of several desserts (see page 230).

Noodles can be made of rice, mung bean, or wheat flour and egg, and they can be almost any length and thickness. They are available fresh and dried (see page 18).

Coconut cream and milk

Thai curries get much of their creaminess from coconut milk and cream, which is not the watery liquid found inside whole coconuts. Canned coconut milk is available, but you will get far better results if you make your own. A simple method of making coconut milk and cream is given on page 17.

Thai Fried Pies

2 cups all-purpose flour

½ teaspoon salt

½ cup vegetable shortening

2 tablespoons cold water

about 3 cups peanut oil, for deep-frying

Hot Sweet Sauce (see page 246), to serve

Filling

2 cups cubed pumpkin

1 cup coconut milk

1 tablespoon vegetarian nam pla (fish sauce) or soy sauce

1 lemon grass stalk, thinly sliced

1 kaffir lime leaf, torn

1 teaspoon crushed dried chilies

1 teaspoon Red Curry Paste (see page 12)

½ red bell pepper, cored, seeded, and diced

½ onion, finely chopped

3 tablespoons finely diced cooked carrot

3 tablespoons finely diced canned water chestnuts

make the filling. Put the pumpkin, coconut milk, nam pla or soy sauce, lemon grass, lime leaf, and crushed dried chilies in a saucepan and bring to a boil. Reduce the heat and simmer for about 15 minutes, or until the pumpkin is tender. Mash the mixture in the pan and continue to simmer if you think it is too thin—it should be fairly thick. Remove from the heat and allow to cool.

meanwhile, make the pastry. Sift the flour and salt into a bowl. Cut the fat into small pieces and add to the flour, a little at a time, blending it in with your fingertips until the mixture resembles fine bread crumbs. Add the measurement water and stir with a knife until it is incorporated. Knead the mixture quickly until a dough is formed, then wrap in foil and chill in the refrigerator for 10–15 minutes.

add the remaining filling ingredients to the cold pumpkin mixture and mix together.

roll out the chilled dough thinly, and cut it into 16 rounds, each 3 inches across. Divide the filling equally between the pastry rounds, fold over to enclose and seal with a fork.

heat the oil in a wok or deep skillet to 350–375°F, or until a cube of bread browns in 30 seconds. Deep-fry the pies, in 2 batches, for 5–6 minutes until golden brown. Remove with a slotted spoon and drain on paper towels.

serve the pies hot or warm, with the hot sweet sauce in a separate bowl.

Makes 16
Preparation time: *about 40 minutes, plus chilling*
Cooking time: *35–40 minutes*

Forest Curry with Litchis

Canned litchis are widely available, so even if you cannot find fresh ones, you can still make this curry. You can also use rambutans instead of litchis.

2½ cups water

1 tablespoon Red Curry Paste (see page 12)

20 fresh litchis, seeded, or 1 lb can litchis, drained and juice reserved

1¼ teaspoons salt

4 small round eggplants, quartered

½ cup green beans, chopped into 1 inch lengths

6 kaffir lime leaves, torn

¾ oz krachai or 3 inch piece of fresh galangal, peeled and sliced

4 baby corn

2 tablespoons green peppercorns

2 large fresh green chilies

2 teaspoons palm sugar or light brown sugar

½ cup diced cucumber

heat the measurement water in a saucepan, add the curry paste and stir to blend thoroughly. If you are using canned litchis, add the reserved juice now, then add the salt and bring the mixture to a boil, stirring.

reduce the heat to a slow boil and add all the remaining ingredients, except the litchis and cucumber. Cook, stirring, for 30 seconds.

add the litchis and cucumber and cook, stirring occasionally, for 3–4 minutes. Serve immediately.

Serves 4
Preparation time: *10 minutes*
Cooking time: *about 8 minutes*

clipboard: Krachai, which has a stronger flavor than galangal and ginger, is more often available dried in packages, but you may come across the fresh root in some Asian markets.

Green Curry with Straw Mushrooms

Green curry paste is made from crushed fresh green chilies and herbs, and it is usually hot. Although you can buy canned and bottled pastes, it is easy to make your own.

1¼ cups coconut milk

3 tablespoons Green Curry Paste (see page 13)

1¼ cups Vegetable Stock (see page 15)

4 small round eggplants, each cut into 8 pieces

3 tablespoons palm sugar or light brown sugar

1 teaspoon salt

4 teaspoons vegetarian nam pla (fish sauce) or soy sauce

1 oz krachai or 3 inch piece of fresh galangal, peeled and sliced

14 oz can straw mushrooms, drained

¼ green bell pepper, cored, seeded, and thinly sliced

To garnish

handful of fresh basil leaves

2 tablespoons coconut milk

heat the coconut milk in a saucepan, add the curry paste and stir to blend thoroughly. Add the stock and then the eggplants, sugar, salt, nam pla or soy sauce, krachai or galangal, and mushrooms. Bring to a boil and cook, stirring, for 2 minutes. Add the bell pepper, reduce the heat and cook for 1 minute.

serve in a bowl, garnished with the basil leaves and drizzled with the coconut milk.

Serves 4
Preparation time: *7 minutes*
Cooking time: *8 minutes*

clipboard: Asian eggplants can be either long, thin, and pink, small, round, and pale green or tiny, round, and darker green. They are often available in large supermarkets and Asian markets. If you substitute the large purple-black variety more commonly found in Western stores, remember that they cook faster than the Asian types, so adjust your cooking times accordingly.

Yellow Curry with Carrots

⅔ cup Vegetable Stock (see page 15)

5 kaffir lime leaves

3 inch piece of fresh galangal, peeled and sliced

2 carrots, cut into chunks

4 garlic cloves, crushed

2 large fresh chilies (red and green)

1 tablespoon peanut oil

2 tablespoons Crushed Roasted Nuts (see page 248)

1¼ cups coconut milk

2 tablespoons Yellow Curry Paste (see page 13)

8 canned, drained straw mushrooms

4 shallots

½ teaspoon salt, or to taste

put the stock in a saucepan, add the lime leaves, galangal, carrots, half the garlic, and the whole chilies and simmer gently for 15 minutes. Strain the stock, reserving the liquid and both the carrots and chilies separately.

heat the oil in a wok or large skillet and stir-fry the remaining garlic over a moderate heat for 1 minute. Add the reserved carrots and the nuts and stir-fry for 1 minute. Add the coconut milk and curry paste and stir until well blended. Add the reserved liquid and the whole mushrooms and shallots and simmer, stirring occasionally, for 15 minutes, or until the shallots are tender. Add the salt.

seed and finely slice the reserved cooked chilies. Serve the curry garnished with the sliced chilies.

Serves 4
Preparation time: *15 minutes*
Cooking time: *35–40 minutes*

clipboard: Turmeric, which gives yellow curry paste its vibrant color, comes from a rhizome, which has to be pounded or grated before it can be used. The dried ground form is an acceptable substitute for fresh turmeric—2 teaspoons ground turmeric and 1 teaspoon palm sugar is the equivalent of 1 oz freshly grated turmeric.

Pork and Beef

Pork with Salted Eggs and Bean Sprouts

Salted eggs take a couple of weeks to prepare, so this is not a dish to make on the spur of the moment! It would make a filling dish for a supper party.

2½ cups water

⅓ cup salt

2 eggs

2 tablespoons vegetable oil

1 garlic clove, chopped

3 oz ground pork

1 tablespoon oyster sauce

1 teaspoon palm sugar or light brown sugar

4 tablespoons Chicken Stock (see page 14)

1 tablespoon nam pla (fish sauce)

4 cups fresh bean sprouts

2 large fresh red chilies, diagonally sliced

1 scallion, diagonally sliced

cilantro leaves, to garnish

heat the measurement water in a saucepan over a moderate heat, add the salt and stir until it dissolves. Remove it from the heat and allow to cool. When it is cool, pour it into a jar and gently add the whole eggs. Put the lid on and allow to stand at room temperature for 15 days. Remove the eggs from the jar and hard-cook. Allow to cool, then shell and halve.

heat the oil in a wok or large skillet and stir-fry the garlic and pork over a moderately high heat for 3 minutes. Add the oyster sauce, sugar, stock, and nam pla and stir-fry for 5 minutes.

add the salted eggs and all the remaining ingredients and cook, stirring, for about 1 minute. Transfer to a serving dish, garnish with cilantro leaves and serve immediately.

Serves 4
Preparation time: *30 minutes, plus cooling and standing*
Cooking time: *20 minutes*

Red Roast Pork

The red coloration from the marinade soaks into the edges of the pork, giving an attractive appearance to this dish.

1½ lb pork shoulder, spare rib or leg, boned and rolled, fat removed

Marinade

2 oz or 1 package red roast pork seasoning mix

1 tablespoon tomato paste

2 tablespoons palm sugar or light brown sugar

1 tablespoon Chicken Stock (see page 14)

To garnish

cilantro leaves

fresh red chilies

make the marinade. Mix all the marinade ingredients together in a bowl. Cut the pork into 4 large pieces, add them to the marinade and turn in the marinade to coat thoroughly. Cover and allow to marinate in the refrigerator for at least 5 hours, preferably overnight.

put the pork in a roasting pan and roast in a preheated oven, 400°F, for 1–1¼ hours, turning occasionally.

slice the pork thinly, arrange it on a serving dish and serve, garnished with cilantro leaves and red chilies.

Serves 4
Preparation time: *10–15 minutes, plus marinating*
Cooking time: *1–1¼ hours*

Pork Satay

You can use oiled metal skewers for this satay or, more traditionally, bamboo skewers, which should be soaked in water for at least an hour before they are needed to help stop them splintering and scorching.

1 lb pork tenderloin

1 teaspoon salt

2 teaspoons palm sugar or light brown sugar

1 teaspoon ground turmeric

1 teaspoon ground coriander

1 teaspoon ground cumin

¾ cup coconut milk

chili powder, for sprinkling

cilantro sprigs, to garnish

lemon slices, to serve

Peanut sauce

½ cup unsalted peanuts, dry-fried

1 teaspoon salt

1¼ cups coconut milk

2 teaspoons Red Curry Paste (see page 12)

2 tablespoons palm sugar or light brown sugar

½ teaspoon lemon juice

cut the pork into 2 inch strips and put it in a large bowl. Add the salt, sugar, turmeric, ground coriander, cumin, and 4 tablespoons of the coconut milk. Mix thoroughly, using your hands to knead the spices into the meat. Cover and allow to marinate in the refrigerator for at least 2 hours.

make the sauce. Put the peanuts and salt in a mortar and grind with a pestle to a thick cream. Set aside. Put half the remaining coconut milk in a saucepan with the curry paste. Heat gently for 3 minutes, stirring constantly. Stir in the ground peanuts with the sugar, lemon juice, and the remaining coconut milk. Simmer gently for 20–30 minutes, stirring frequently to prevent the sauce from sticking. Transfer to a serving bowl.

thread the marinated pork onto skewers and cook on a barbecue or under a preheated hot broiler for 12–15 minutes, turning them several times and brushing frequently with the marinade. Sprinkle the skewers with chili powder, garnish with cilantro sprigs, and serve with the peanut sauce and some lemon slices.

Serves 4
Preparation time: *15–20 minutes, plus marinating*
Cooking time: *about 45 minutes*

Pork with Hot Sauces

12 oz pork tenderloin

½ teaspoon salt

¼ teaspoon ground white pepper

1 tablespoon butter

1 tablespoon vegetable oil

3 garlic cloves

½ inch piece of fresh gingerroot, peeled and chopped

2 fresh red chilies, chopped

1½ teaspoons ground cumin

½ cucumber, finely diced, to serve

Chili and ginger sauce

2 fresh red chilies

1 inch piece of fresh gingerroot, peeled and chopped

½ onion, grated

salt

Tomato and chili sauce

2 tomatoes, skinned and chopped

2 garlic cloves, crushed

pinch of palm sugar or light brown sugar

1 teaspoon hot chili powder

salt

slice the pork thinly and rub with the salt and pepper. Heat the butter and oil in a wok or large skillet and stir-fry the pork over a moderate heat until lightly browned. Remove from the pan and keep warm.

chop the garlic finely and add to the pan with the ginger, chilies, and cumin. Stir-fry for 2 minutes, then return the pork to the pan. Stir-fry for 2 minutes over a low heat, or until the meat is cooked through and tender. If necessary, add a sprinkling of water to keep the meat moist.

make the chili and ginger sauce. Put all the sauce ingredients in a mortar and pound with a pestle to a smooth paste.

make the tomato and chili sauce. Mix all the sauce ingredients together in a small bowl and season with salt to taste.

serve the stir-fried pork with the cucumber and the 2 hot sauces.

Serves 4
Preparation time: *15 minutes*
Cooking time: *8–10 minutes*

Broiled Beef with Spicy Sauce

This dish is from the north of Thailand, an area known as Issan. The food from here is greatly influenced by Laotian cuisine.

10 oz porterhouse steak

Spicy sauce
½ tomato, finely chopped

¼ red onion, finely chopped

1 tablespoon ground chili

6 tablespoons nam pla (fish sauce)

2 tablespoons lime juice or tamarind water (see page 32)

2 teaspoons palm sugar or light brown sugar

1 teaspoon Ground Roast Rice (see page 248)

1 tablespoon Chicken Stock (see page 14)

To garnish
basil sprigs

flat leaf parsley sprigs

cilantro leaves

fresh red and green chilies

put the steak under a preheated hot broiler and cook, turning it once, according to your taste.

while the meat is cooking, make the sauce. Mix all the sauce ingredients together in a bowl.

when the beef is ready, slice it up, arrange the pieces on a serving dish and garnish with the basil and parsley sprigs, cilantro leaves, and chilies. Serve the sauce separately.

Serves 4
Preparation time: *10 minutes*
Cooking time: *6 minutes (for medium-rare)*

clipboard: If you cannot find Thai or holy basil to use in Thai cooking, it is fine to use ordinary (European) basil, which has a sweeter flavor.

Thai Green Beef Curry

This green curry dish is typical of the cuisine of the central plains. Pork, chicken, or duck can be used instead of beef.

2 tablespoons peanut oil

1 inch piece of fresh gingerroot, peeled and finely chopped

2 shallots, chopped

4 tablespoons Green Curry Paste (see page 13)

1 lb beef tenderloin, cubed

1¼ cups coconut milk

4 tablespoons nam pla (fish sauce)

1 teaspoon palm sugar or light brown sugar

3 kaffir lime leaves, finely chopped, or ¼ teaspoon grated lime zest

2 teaspoons tamarind water (see page 32)

1 fresh green chili, seeded and finely sliced

salt and pepper

boiled rice, to serve

To garnish

1 yellow bell pepper, cored, seeded and cut into strips

fried chopped garlic (optional)

fresh red chili, seeded, cut into very fine strips, and curled (optional—see page 148)

heat the oil in a wok or large skillet and stir-fry the ginger and shallots over a low heat for about 3 minutes, or until softened. Add the curry paste and stir-fry for 2 minutes.

add the beef to the pan, stir until it is evenly coated in the spice mixture and stir-fry for 3 minutes to seal the meat. Stir in the coconut milk and bring it to a boil. Reduce the heat and cook the curry over a low heat, stirring occasionally, for about 10 minutes, or until the meat is cooked through and the sauce has thickened.

stir in the nam pla, sugar, lime leaves or lime zest, tamarind water, and chili. Cook the curry for a further 5 minutes, then season to taste.

serve the curry hot with boiled rice, garnished with yellow pepper strips and fried garlic, and topped with a red chili curl, if desired.

Serves 4
Preparation time: *10 minutes*
Cooking time: *25 minutes*

Beef and Galangal Salad

Sticky (glutinous) rice, which is widely used in the dishes of the north and northeast of Thailand, is a type of short-grain rice that is gluten free.

10 oz ground beef

2 tablespoons Ground Roast Rice—use sticky (glutinous) rice (see page 248)

5 thin slices of fresh galangal or gingerroot

3 tablespoons finely chopped scallion

1 teaspoon ground chili

3–4 tablespoons lemon juice

3 tablespoons nam pla (fish sauce)

½ teaspoon palm sugar or light brown sugar

4–5 mint sprigs, leaves chopped, plus extra sprigs to garnish

3 tablespoons chopped shallots

1 crisp lettuce, separated into leaves, to serve

put the ground beef in a saucepan and cook over a low heat for 10–15 minutes, stirring constantly, until the meat is broken up, cooked and all the liquid has been absorbed. Transfer the beef to a bowl, stir in all the remaining ingredients, except the lettuce, and mix well.

arrange a bed of lettuce on a shallow dish and top with the beef mixture. Garnish with mint sprigs and serve immediately.

Serves 4
Preparation time: *10 minutes*
Cooking time: *10–15 minutes*

Chiang Mai Jungle Curry with Beef

2 tablespoons peanut oil

1 lb lean beef, thinly sliced

1¾ cups coconut milk

salt and pepper

Spice paste

2 tablespoons yellow bean sauce

3 tablespoons Red Curry Paste (see page 12)

2 tablespoons palm sugar or light brown sugar

4 shallots, chopped

2 garlic cloves, chopped

2 large fresh red chilies, seeded and chopped

1 lemon grass stalk, chopped, or ¼ teaspoon grated lemon zest

1 inch piece of fresh galangal or gingerroot, peeled and chopped

½ teaspoon dried shrimp paste

4 tablespoons lime juice

boiled rice, to serve

To garnish

½ red bell pepper, cored, seeded, and cut into fine strips

2 scallions, cut into very fine strips

make the spice paste. Put all the paste ingredients in a food processor and process to a thick paste. Alternatively, put them in a mortar and pound with a pestle.

heat the oil in a large, flameproof casserole and stir-fry the beef over a moderate heat for 3 minutes to seal the meat. Add the spice paste and stir-fry for a further 3 minutes.

pour the coconut milk into the casserole, stir to mix and bring to a boil. Reduce the heat, cover and simmer the curry gently, stirring occasionally, for 50 minutes, or until the beef is tender. Season to taste.

serve the curry hot with boiled rice, garnished with fine strips of red bell pepper and very fine strips of scallion.

Serves 3
Preparation time: *15 minutes*
Cooking time: *about 1 hour*

Beef and Bamboo Shoot Salad

Bamboo shoots are readily available in cans, when they are peeled and partially cooked. You can also sometimes find fresh or vacuum-packed shoots in large stores.

8 oz tenderloin or sirloin steak, thinly sliced

¾ cup coconut milk

8 oz can bamboo shoots, drained and sliced

1½ tablespoons Red Curry Paste (see page 12)

2 tablespoons chopped lemon grass

1½ teaspoons finely grated lemon zest

2 tablespoons lemon juice

1½ teaspoons nam pla (fish sauce)

3 small fresh red bird's eye chilies, finely sliced into rings

1 lettuce, separated into leaves, to serve

To garnish

shredded scallion

finely sliced kaffir lime leaves (optional)

put the steak in a small saucepan with the coconut milk and cook over a low heat for 10–15 minutes, or until the steak is tender and has absorbed most of the coconut milk. (Any liquid remaining in the pan should have an oily appearance.) Remove the pan from the heat and allow to cool.

transfer the meat to a bowl. Add all the remaining ingredients, except the chili and lettuce, and mix well.

arrange a bed of lettuce on a shallow serving dish, top with the beef mixture and scatter over the chili. Garnish with shredded scallion and finely sliced lime leaves, if desired. Serve immediately.

Serves 4
Preparation time: *15 minutes*
Cooking time: *10–15 minutes*

Hot Thai Beef Salad

2 tablespoons vegetable oil

500 g (1 lb) sirloin or tenderloin steak, cut across the grain into thin strips

2 garlic cloves, finely chopped

2 fresh green chilies, finely sliced into rings

juice of 2 lemons

1 tablespoon nam pla (fish sauce)

2 teaspoons superfine sugar

2 ripe papayas, peeled, seeded, and finely sliced

½ large cucumber, cut into matchsticks

1½ cups fresh bean sprouts

1 crisp lettuce, shredded

Chili sauce

8 fresh red chilies, chopped

4 garlic cloves, crushed

1 tablespoon nam pla (fish sauce)

2 teaspoons palm sugar or light brown sugar

2 tablespoons lime or lemon juice

¼ teaspoon salt

½ cup water

2 tablespoons peanut oil

make the sauce. Put the chilies, garlic, nam pla, sugar, lime or lemon juice, and salt in a small saucepan. Stir in the measurement water and oil. Bring to a boil, then reduce the heat and simmer for 10–15 minutes. Transfer to a food processor or blender and process until smooth. Transfer to a serving bowl.

heat the oil in a wok or large skillet and stir-fry the steak, garlic, and chilies over a high heat for 3–4 minutes, or until the steak is browned on all sides.

pour in the lemon juice and nam pla, add the sugar and stir-fry for 1–2 minutes.

remove the pan from the heat. Lift the steak out of the liquid with a slotted spoon and toss with the papayas, cucumber, bean sprouts, and lettuce in a large serving bowl. Drizzle the liquid from the pan over the salad ingredients as a dressing and serve hot with the chili sauce.

Serves 4
Preparation time: *10 minutes*
Cooking time: *about 20 minutes*

Chicken and Duck

Phuket Chicken and Lemon Grass Curry

3 tablespoons vegetable oil

4 garlic cloves, crushed

3 shallots, chopped

3 lemon grass stalks, finely chopped, or ¾ teaspoon grated lemon zest

6 kaffir lime leaves, shredded, or ¼ teaspoon grated lime zest

3 tablespoons Green Curry Paste (see page 13)

1 tablespoon nam pla (fish sauce)

2 teaspoons palm sugar or light brown sugar

1 cup Chicken Stock (see page 14)

8 large chicken drumsticks

salt and pepper (optional)

noodles, to serve

To garnish

1 fresh red chili, diagonally sliced

kaffir lime leaves (optional)

lemon grass stalks, tied in a knot (optional)

heat the oil in a wok or large skillet and stir-fry the garlic and shallots over a low heat for 3 minutes, or until softened.

add the lemon grass or lemon zest, lime leaves or lime zest, curry paste, nam pla, and sugar to the pan and stir-fry for 1 minute, then add the stock and chicken drumsticks and bring the curry to a boil. Reduce the heat, cover and simmer gently, stirring occasionally, for 40–45 minutes until the chicken is tender and cooked through.

taste and adjust the seasoning, if necessary. Serve the curry hot with noodles, garnished with the sliced red chili, and lime leaves and knotted lemon grass stalks, if desired.

Serves 4
Preparation time: *15 minutes*
Cooking time: *about 1 hour*

Ground Chicken with Basil

5 small fresh green chilies

2 garlic cloves

2 tablespoons vegetable oil

4 oz ground chicken

1 shallot, chopped

¼ cup bamboo shoots

2 tablespoons chopped red bell pepper

1½ tablespoons diced carrot

1 teaspoon palm sugar or light brown sugar

3 tablespoons nam pla (fish sauce)

3 tablespoons Chicken Stock (see page 14)

¼ cup finely chopped basil leaves

boiled rice, to serve

To garnish
Crispy Garlic (see page 250)

Crispy Shallots (see page 250)

Crispy Basil (see page 248)

put the chilies and garlic into a mortar and pound together with a pestle until well broken down.

heat the oil in a wok or large skillet and stir-fry the chilies and garlic over a moderate heat for 30 seconds. Add all the remaining ingredients and stir-fry for 4 minutes. Increase the heat to high and stir-fry for a further 30 seconds.

turn the stir-fry onto a serving dish and serve with boiled rice, garnished with crispy garlic, crispy shallots, and crispy basil.

Serves 4
Preparation time: *10 minutes*
Cooking time: *6 minutes*

clipboard: Thai cooks usually flavor their oil with garlic and shallots before using it. The crispy garlic and shallots are removed from the oil, reserved and then sprinkled over many different dishes. If you like, you can deep-fry just garlic or just shallots, or you can deep-fry them both, then store them together rather than separately.

Stir-fried Chicken with Cashew Nuts and Baby Corn

This Chinese-influenced dish looks impressive but is easy to prepare.

3 tablespoons vegetable oil

4 oz boneless chicken, skinned and cut into bite-size pieces

¼ onion, sliced

2 oz baby corn, diagonally sliced

⅓ cup cashew nuts

½ cup soy sauce

4 tablespoons Chicken Stock (see page 14)

4 teaspoons palm sugar or light brown sugar

1 tablespoon scallion, diagonally sliced

pepper

1 large fresh red chili, diagonally sliced, to garnish

heat the oil in a wok or large skillet and stir-fry the chicken, onion, baby corn, and cashew nuts over a high heat for 3 minutes.

reduce the heat and stir in the soy sauce. Then add the stock, sugar, and scallion and season with pepper. Increase the heat and stir-fry for a further 2 minutes.

turn the stir-fry onto a serving dish, sprinkle with the sliced red chili and serve immediately.

Serves 4
Preparation time: *10 minutes*
Cooking time: *5–6 minutes*

Thai Touches

Nam pla

One of the most important elements in Thai cooking is the fish sauce that is called nam pla in Thailand. The Vietnamese equivalent, nuoc naam, is almost identical and can be used in all recipes that require nam pla. The sauce is pungent and salty and often replaces most or all of the salt that a Western cook would automatically add to a dish.

As well as being included in recipes, however, nam pla can be offered, straight from the bottle, as a dipping sauce in a small bowl, garnished with two or three finely chopped small chilies and a dash of lime juice.

Chili sauce

After nam pla, chili sauce is the most popular of all dipping sauces. A basic recipe is given on page 138, but it is possible to buy ready-made sauces that vary in strength and intensity. If you make your own, aim to balance the spicy, salty, and sour flavors of the ingredients. Offer neatly chopped raw vegetables, such as cucumbers, cabbag,e and green beans, pieces of cooked eggplant or sweet potato, slices of omelet, portions of grilled fish or meat, and even fruit to dip into a dish of your own sauce.

Using chilies

Chilies are included in many of the recipes in this book and are used in amounts that will give an authentic Thai flavor. They are also used as garnishes in many of the recipes, when they are seeded and finely sliced, sometimes on the diagonal for added interest, or used whole, which the unwary should avoid eating as part of the dish. Fine strips of red or green chili can be put into iced water and left for them to curl up, to make an eye-catching garnish.

Green chilies are hotter than the riper red chilies, although this may be something of an illusion, created by the fact that a chili as it ripens becomes sweeter and more rounded in flavor, so the heat is less obvious. Quantities can always be adjusted to suit your personal preferences.

Of the red chilies, smaller chilies tend to be hotter than the larger, more elongated ones. The rounded Scotch bonnet and pointed bird's eye (mouse dropping) chilies pack powerful punches for their size. Among chilies usually available in supermarkets, the Fresno, which ranges in color from glossy green to orange and red, is medium-hot and the jalapeño, though slightly smaller, is another hot one.

Dried chilies are hotter than fresh ones. Just one or two whole small dried red chilies or a small quantity of crushed dried chilies, dried chili flakes or ground chili will add a lot of heat to a recipe.

Scraping the seeds from a chili, as well as removing the white membrane, will reduce its heat, because these are the hottest parts of a chili.

Finally, always handle chilies with care. Wear disposable gloves if your hands are sensitive, and be careful not to touch any part of your face, particularly your eyes, before you have washed your hands.

Using banana leaves as a serving dish adds an authentic touch to cooking Thai food at home. Buy them at large Asian markets.

Using banana leaves

Banana leaves are widely used in Thai cuisine as a way of both cooking and serving food. In addition to adding a touch of the exotic to a meal, the leaf imparts a subtle flavor to the dish, either acting in the same way as a piece of foil when wrapped around a filling and cooked, or used as a serving dish or container, having been cut and shaped (see pages 168 and 234). Whole leaves can be bought, rolled, in packs of four or five from large Asian markets and should be warmed over a flame or electric burner before they are used to lighten the color and soften them. Alternatively, the leaves can be dipped in boiling water, then patted dry with paper towels.

Pandanus leaves, which have a flowery flavor and a strong green color, can be used in the same way as banana leaves.

Creative garnishes

Slivers of fresh coconut, which can also be toasted, or grated fresh coconut make attractive decorations for both sweet and savory Thai dishes (see pages 188 and 238), and wafer-thin ribbons of mooli or cucumber, which can be easily made with a swivel-bladed vegetable peeler, are also effective garnishes (see pages 46 and 176). Flowering chives are another interesting decorative item, and can be used for tying around little won ton pouches (see page 44), while a few lemon grass stalks are sometimes tied together in a knot to provide a finishing touch (see page 142).

Chilies, introduced by the Portuguese in the 16th century are used in very large quantities in Thai cooking.

Coconut Broiled Chicken

The stems and roots of cilantro are used together with the leaves to add flavor Thai dishes. The dried seeds (coriander) are also often used, but are never substituted for the fresh herb.

2–3 boneless chicken breasts

Marinade

1¾ cups coconut milk

4 garlic cloves, finely chopped

4 small fresh green or red chilies, finely chopped

1 inch piece of fresh gingerroot, peeled and sliced

grated zest and juice of 1 lime

2 tablespoons palm sugar or light brown sugar

3 tablespoons soy sauce

1 tablespoon nam pla (fish sauce)

½ cup cilantro leaves, stalks, and roots

Chicken Stock (see page 14), for thinning (optional)

To garnish

1 fresh red chili, seeded and finely diced

very fine strips of scallion

make the marinade. Mix all the marinade ingredients together in a bowl.

make 3 diagonal cuts in each side of the chicken breasts, put them in a dish and pour over the marinade. Cover and allow to marinate in the refrigerator for 2 hours.

arrange the chicken pieces in a foil-lined broiler pan, making sure that they are thickly spread with the marinade, and cook under a preheated hot broiler, turning occasionally, for about 15 minutes, or until cooked through. The skin side will take a little longer to cook than the other side.

meanwhile, put the remaining marinade in a small saucepan, bring to a boil, stirring constantly, adding a little stock if it is too thick, and continue to boil for 2–3 minutes. The sauce must be brought to a high temperature to cook any raw chicken juices.

when the chicken is cooked, cut it into slices and arrange the pieces on a serving dish. Serve the chicken garnished with very fine strips of scallion and diced red chili, with the sauce in a separate bowl.

Serves 4
Preparation time: *10 minutes, plus marinating*
Cooking time: *15 minutes*

Barbecued Chicken

3 lb whole chicken, spatchcocked, or part-boned chicken breasts

2 inch piece of fresh galangal, peeled and finely chopped

4 garlic cloves, crushed

1 large fresh red chili, finely chopped

4 shallots, finely chopped

2 tablespoons finely chopped cilantro leaves

²⁄₃ cup thick coconut milk (see page 17)

salt and pepper

flowering chives, to garnish

To serve

Chili Sauce (see page 138)

boiled sticky (glutinous) rice

lime wedges

rub the chicken all over with salt and pepper and put it in a shallow dish.

put the galangal, garlic, chili, shallots, and cilantro in a food processor and process to a paste. Add the coconut milk and mix until well blended. Pour the marinade over the chicken, cover and allow to marinate in the refrigerator overnight.

remove the chicken from the marinade and cook on a hot barbecue for 30–40 minutes for spatchcocked chicken, or until the juices run clear when a skewer is inserted into one of the legs, and 10–15 minutes for chicken breasts, turning and basting them regularly with the marinade.

leave the chicken to rest for 5 minutes, then chop it into small pieces with a cleaver. Serve with the chili sauce, sticky rice, and lime wedges. Garnish with flowering chives and eat with your fingers.

Serves 3–4
Preparation time: *15 minutes, plus marinating*
Cooking time: *30–40 minutes for spatchcocked chicken;*
10–15 minutes for chicken breasts

Red Curry Duck

This rich dish is very popular in Thailand. It gets its color and flavor from the red curry paste, making it one of the milder curries.

¼ roast duck

1 tablespoon vegetable oil

1½ tablespoons Red Curry Paste (see page 12)

⅔ cup coconut milk

1 tablespoon palm sugar or light brown sugar

3 kaffir lime leaves, torn, or ¼ teaspoon grated lime zest

½ cup peas, fresh or frozen

1 large fresh red chili, diagonally sliced

4 tablespoons Chicken Stock (see page 14)

2 tomatoes, finely diced

1 cup fresh or canned pineapple, cut into chunks, plus extra to serve

1 tablespoon nam pla (fish sauce)

noodles, to serve

To garnish

fine strips of red bell pepper

very fine strips of scallion

remove the skin and meat from the duck, chop them into bite-size pieces and set both the skin and meat aside.

heat the oil in a wok or large skillet and stir-fry the curry paste over a moderate heat for 30 seconds. Add 3 tablespoons of the coconut milk, mix it with the paste, then add the remainder and cook, stirring, over a low heat for 1 minute.

add the duck skin and meat and cook, stirring, for 2 minutes. Add the sugar, lime leaves or lime zest, peas, chili, stock, tomatoes, and pineapple. Mix well, then add the nam pla. Stir thoroughly to combine, then transfer to a serving bowl.

serve with extra pineapple and noodles, garnished with fine strips of bell pepper and very fine strips of scallion.

Serves 3–4
Preparation time: *15 minutes*
Cooking time: *5 minutes*

Fish and Shellfish

Stir-fried Squid with Basil

Take care to cook the squid over a high heat and only briefly, as it can easily turn rubbery in texture if overcooked.

2 tablespoons oil

6 garlic cloves, chopped

12 small fresh green chilies, finely sliced

1–2 shallots, chopped

4 oz squid, cleaned and cut into strips

½ green bell pepper, cored, seeded, and chopped

2 tablespoons Fish Stock (see page 15)

1 tablespoon nam pla (fish sauce)

1 tablespoon palm sugar or light brown sugar

¼ cup basil leaves

1 tablespoon Crispy Shallots (see page 250), to garnish

heat the oil in a wok or large skillet and stir-fry the garlic, chilies, and shallots over a moderate heat for 30 seconds.

add the squid and bell pepper, increase the heat to high and stir-fry for 1 minute, then reduce the heat and add the stock, nam pla, and basil. Cook, stirring, for 1 minute.

serve immediately, garnished with the crispy shallots.

Serves 2
Preparation time: *8 minutes*
Cooking time: *3–4 minutes*

Broiled Fish in Ginger and Oyster Sauce

1 whole gray mullet, cleaned

½ tablespoon Garlic Mixture (see page 250)

½ onion, chopped

5 mushrooms, sliced

2 tablespoons finely sliced fresh gingerroot

1 celery stick, sliced

1 teaspoon pepper

1 tablespoon soy sauce

1 tablespoon oyster sauce

1 cup Fish Stock (see page 15)

lemon slices, to garnish

score the skin of the mullet with a sharp knife to allow the sauce to be absorbed during cooking. Rub the fish with the garlic mixture, pressing it well into the cuts. Transfer the fish to a shallow heatproof dish.

mix the remaining ingredients together in a bowl and pour the mixture over the fish. Cook under a preheated moderate broiler for 20 minutes, turning the fish over halfway through the cooking time.

carefully transfer the fish to a warm serving dish, pour over the sauce, garnish with lemon slices and serve immediately.

Serves 2
Preparation time: *20 minutes*
Cooking time: *20 minutes*

clipboard: Snapper can be used instead in this recipe if you cannot find mullet.

Fish with Tamarind Water and Ginger

2 whole gray mullet or mackerel, cleaned

4 shallots, chopped

1 tablespoon dried shrimp paste

1 teaspoon pepper

3 cups water

2 tablespoons finely chopped fresh gingerroot

2 tablespoons tamarind water (see page 32)

4 tablespoons nam pla (fish sauce)

3 tablespoons palm sugar or light brown sugar

4 scallions, chopped, plus extra to garnish

To serve

boiled rice

pickled chilies (optional)

remove the head and tail from each mullet or mackerel and cut the fish lengthwise in half. Score the skin with a sharp knife to allow the sauce to be absorbed during cooking.

put the shallots, shrimp paste, and pepper in a food processor and process to a paste. Alternatively, pound in a mortar with a pestle. Stir the paste into the measurement water in a saucepan large enough to hold the pieces of fish and bring it to a boil.

add the fish, ginger, tamarind water, nam pla, sugar, and scallions. Reduce the heat and simmer for about 20 minutes.

serve the fish hot with boiled rice and pickled chilies, if desired, and garnished with chopped scallions.

Serves 4
Preparation time: *20 minutes*
Cooking time: *25 minutes*

Steamed Butterfish with Lemon Grass

Sometimes known as pomfret, butterfish is a deep-bodied but thin fish, popular for its firm, white flesh, which comes easily away from the bones. Use any flat fish instead if necessary.

12 oz whole butterfish, cleaned

1 teaspoon salt

1 lemon grass stalk, cut into 3 pieces

15 small fresh red and green chilies

1 fresh cilantro root, crushed and chopped

3 garlic cloves, finely sliced

3 tablespoons nam pla (fish sauce)

2 tablespoons soy sauce

ground chili, to serve

cut diagonal slashes into each side of the fish and rub the salt all over to firm it up. Leave for 2 minutes, then wash off the salt.

put the fish on a plate, arrange the lemon grass on top, then put it into a steamer. Steam for 35–40 minutes.

meanwhile, chop the chilies very finely and put them into a small bowl with the cilantro, garlic, nam pla, and soy sauce. Stir thoroughly.

pour the sauce over the fish and serve with the ground chili on the side.

Serves 3–4
Preparation time: *5 minutes*
Cooking time: *35–40 minutes*

clipboard: Supermarkets generally sell lemon grass in packs of 4–6 stalks. Before use, the straw-like tops need to be trimmed as well as the ends, and sometimes the outside leaves are very woody and need to be removed. Dried and ground lemon grass is also available, or you can use lemon zest or juice instead.

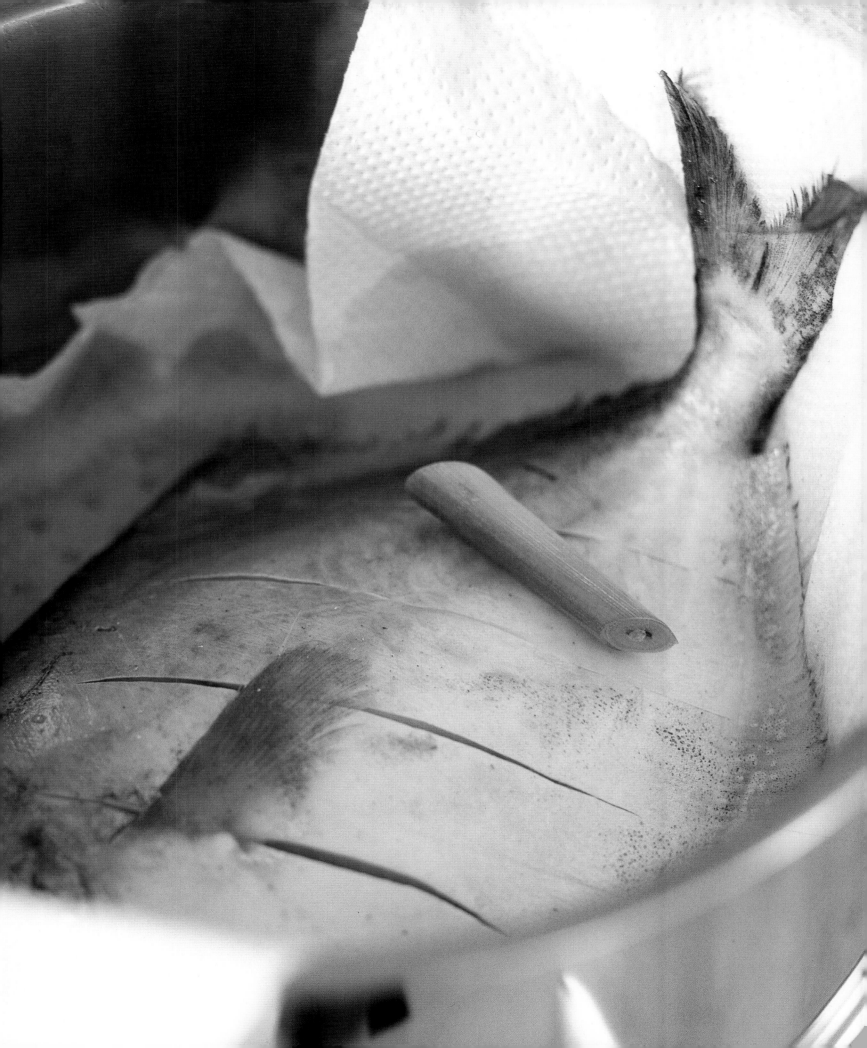

Fish in Garlic Sauce

John Dory is a deep-bodied fish with firm white flesh that comes easily away from the bones. It makes an unusual alternative in this highly flavored dish.

1 whole mullet, lemon sole, porgy, or John Dory, cleaned

vegetable oil, for deep-frying, plus 3 tablespoons

2 tablespoons Garlic Mixture (see page 250)

2 tablespoons nam pla (fish sauce)

1 teaspoon palm sugar or light brown sugar

2 celery sticks, thinly sliced

To garnish

cilantro sprigs

1 fresh red chili, cut into fine strips.

neatly score the skin of the fish diagonally in both directions to allow the sauce to be absorbed during cooking. Pat dry with paper towels.

heat the oil for deep-frying in a wok or large skillet to 350–375°F, or until a cube of bread browns in 30 seconds. Deep-fry the fish for 10–15 minutes until golden brown, turning halfway through the cooking time. Remove with a slotted spoon and drain on paper towels.

meanwhile, heat the 3 tablespoons oil in a saucepan large enough to hold the whole fish. Stir in the garlic mixture and cook, stirring, until it changes color. Stir in the nam pla and sugar. Add the fish to the pan, turning until well coated in the mixture.

transfer the fish to a serving dish and keep warm. Add the celery to the sauce remaining in the pan and stir-fry for 2 minutes, then pour the mixture over the fish. Garnish with cilantro sprigs and fine strips of red chili. Serve warm.

Serves 4
Preparation time: *15 minutes*
Cooking time: *20 minutes*

Spicy Fishcakes

If you prefer, you can replace half the cod fillet with 8 oz raw jumbo shrimp, peeled and deveined, to make spicy shrimp cakes instead.

1 lb cod fillet, skinned and cut into chunks

3 tablespoons Red Curry Paste (see page 12)

1 egg

3 tablespoons nam pla (fish sauce)

1–2 tablespoons rice flour

¾ cup thin green beans, finely chopped

1 tablespoon finely shredded kaffir lime leaves or ¼ teaspoon grated lime zest

oil, for deep-frying

To serve

Chili Sauce (see page 138)

lime slices

cucumber salad (optional)

put the cod and curry paste in a food processor and process to a thick paste. Alternatively, put in a mortar and pound with a pestle.

transfer the fish mixture to a bowl and add the egg, nam pla, and enough of the flour to knead with your hands into a stiff mixture. Work in the green beans and lime leaves or lime zest.

form the fish mixture into 16–20 balls and, using your hands, flatten each ball into a round about ½ inch thick.

heat the oil in a wok or deep skillet to 350–375°F, or until a cube of bread browns in 30 seconds. Deep-fry the fishcakes, a few at a time, for 4–5 minutes on each side until cooked and golden brown. Take care not to overcook them. Remove the fishcakes with a slotted spoon and drain on paper towels. Serve hot with the chili sauce, lime slices, and a cucumber salad, if desired.

Serves 4–5
Preparation time: *20 minutes*
Cooking time: *16–20 minutes*

Crab Curry

If you cannot find crab claws, use 1 lb raw peeled and deveined jumbo shrimp instead.

1 tablespoon vegetable oil

1½ teaspoons Red Curry Paste (see page 12)

6 tablespoons coconut milk

1 kaffir lime leaf, torn

12 raw crab claws

⅔ cup Fish Stock (see page 15)

2 tablespoons palm sugar or light brown sugar

1 teaspoon salt

½ cup bamboo shoots

To garnish

½ large fresh red chili, diagonally sliced

cilantro leaves

heat the oil in a wok or large skillet and stir-fry the curry paste over a moderately high heat for 30 seconds. Add all the remaining ingredients, stir well and simmer for 10 minutes. If the liquid level reduces significantly, add more stock.

turn the mixture into a serving bowl and serve, garnished with the sliced red chili and cilantro leaves.

Serves 3–4
Preparation time: *3 minutes*
Cooking time: *12 minutes*

clipboard: Kaffir lime leaves add a fragrant citrus flavor to Thai dishes. They are available dried from large supermarkets, but can be bought fresh in Asian markets. If they are unavailable, use lime zest or juice.

Fresh Crab Curry with Chilies

For added impact, you can serve the curry in the crab shell from the fresh crab. Wash the crab shell and dry thoroughly with paper towels before using.

1 teaspoon curry powder

1 cup water

1 lb raw crabmeat (see below)

4 scallions, chopped

2 fresh red chilies, seeded and finely sliced

1½ teaspoons palm sugar or light brown sugar

1 tablespoon white wine

½ teaspoon salt

¼ teaspoon pepper

1 egg

1 tablespoon light cream

To garnish

dried mango slices

prawn crackers

fresh red chilies, sliced into rings

mix the curry powder with the measurement water in a saucepan and bring to a boil. Stir in the crabmeat.

return to a boil and add the scallions, chilies, sugar, wine, salt, and pepper. Reduce the heat and simmer for 10 minutes.

meanwhile, mix the egg and cream together in a small bowl. Beat in 2 tablespoons of the curry sauce and return the mixture to the saucepan. Cook, stirring, over a low heat for 1 minute.

transfer the crab to a serving bowl and garnish with dried mango slices, prawn cracker,s and sliced red chilies.

Serves 4
Preparation time: *15 minutes*
Cooking time: *15–20 minutes*

clipboard: To prepare the crabmeat, remove the legs and claws from the crab. Remove the undershell and discard the gills. Clean the body and cut the meat into small chunks. Crack the legs and claws and extract the meat.

Shrimp Vermicelli

Although it seems fiddly, using salt pork instead of vegetable oil imparts a highly distinctive flavor to this dish.

2 oz salt pork

8 tablespoons milk

1 teaspoon dark soy sauce

3 tablespoons oyster sauce

1 teaspoon chopped garlic

5 black peppercorns, crushed

¼ cup cilantro leaves, stalks, and roots, plus extra leaves to garnish

3 inch piece of fresh gingerroot, peeled and cut into fine matchsticks

4 oz dried glass noodles, soaked in hot water for about 15 minutes and drained

12 raw shrimps, peeled, but tails left intact

2 tablespoons Fish Stock (see page 15—optional)

heat the fat in a wok or large skillet over a moderate heat until the oil runs, stirring occasionally. Remove the wok from the heat and set aside. Discard the fat, but leave the oil in the wok to cool for about 5 minutes.

meanwhile, combine the milk, soy sauce, and oyster sauce in a bowl.

when the oil has cooled, add the garlic, crushed peppercorns, cilantro, and ginger and stir-fry for 30 seconds. Add the noodles and milk mixture, stir together thoroughly over a high heat, then reduce the heat to low, cover and cook for 12 minutes.

increase the heat, add the shrimp, and the stock if the sauce looks too thick, and cook, stirring, for about 2–3 minutes until the shrimp have turned pink and are cooked through.

turn the mixture into a serving bowl and serve immediately, garnished with cilantro leaves.

Serves 4
Preparation time: *10 minutes*
Cooking time: *20 minutes*

Thai Red Shrimp and Cucumber Curry

2 tablespoons peanut oil

I shallot, chopped

2 garlic cloves, chopped

2 tablespoons Red Curry Paste (see page 12)

I fresh red chili, seeded and chopped

3 kaffir lime leaves, finely shredded, or ¼ teaspoon grated lime zest

I¼ cups coconut milk

20 raw jumbo shrimp, peeled and deveined

¾ cucumber, halved lengthwise, seeded and thickly sliced

I tablespoon nam pla (fish sauce)

I teaspoon palm sugar or light brown sugar

noodles, to serve

To garnish (optional)

shredded kaffir lime leaves

cucumber ribbons

heat the oil in a wok or large skillet and stir-fry the shallot and garlic over a low heat for about 3 minutes until softened. Add the curry paste, chili, and lime leaves or lime zest and stir-fry for an additional minute.

add the coconut milk, increase the heat and bring the sauce to a boil, then reduce the heat and simmer the sauce gently, stirring occasionally, for 5 minutes.

add the shrimp, cucumber, nam pla, and sugar to the pan. Stir to coat the ingredients evenly in the sauce, then simmer the curry gently for 5 minutes, or until the shrimp have turned pink and are cooked through and the cucumber is tender. Taste and adjust the seasoning, if necessary.

serve the curry hot with noodles, garnished with shredded lime leaves and cucumber ribbons, if desired.

Serves 4
Preparation time: *10 minutes*
Cooking time: *15 minutes*

Shrimp in Coconut Sauce

Although nam pla has an extremely pungent flavor,

its distinctive taste is characteristic of many traditional

Thai dishes, including seafood ones.

16 raw jumbo shrimp

2 tablespoons vegetable oil

1 large onion, finely chopped

2 lemon grass stalks, chopped, plus extra whole stalks to garnish (optional)

2 fresh red chilies, sliced

1 inch piece of fresh gingerroot, peeled and shredded

1 tablespoon ground cumin

1 tablespoon ground coriander

2 tablespoons nam pla (fish sauce)

1 cup thick coconut milk (see page 17)

3 tablespoons Crushed Roasted Nuts (see page 248)

2 tomatoes, skinned and chopped

1 teaspoon palm sugar or light brown sugar

To serve

1 tablespoon lime juice

cilantro leaves, chopped

peel the shrimp, leaving the tails intact. Remove the dark vein running along the back.

heat the oil in a wok or large skillet and stir-fry the onion over a moderate heat for 1 minute, or until soft and golden. Add the chopped lemon grass, chilies, ginger, cumin, and ground coriander and stir-fry for 2 minutes.

add the nam pla and coconut milk to the pan. Stir well and then add the nuts and tomatoes. Cook, stirring occasionally, over a low heat until the tomatoes are soft and the flavors of the sauce are well developed.

stir in the shrimp and simmer gently for 5 minutes, or until they have turned pink and are cooked through. Add the sugar and transfer to a warm serving dish.

serve hot, sprinkled with lime juice and chopped cilantro, and garnished with lemon grass stalks, if desired.

Serves 4
Preparation time: *20 minutes*
Cooking time: *20 minutes*

Green Spicy Shrimp Curry

3 cups coconut milk

2 tablespoons Green Curry Paste (see page 13)

2 teaspoons ground galangal

1½ lb raw large shrimp

2 tablespoons nam pla (fish sauce)

boiled rice, to serve (optional)

To garnish

kaffir lime leaves

4 basil leaves, shredded

put the coconut milk in a pitcher and chill in the refrigerator for at least 1 hour, or until the thick milk rises to the surface. Scoop 1 cup off the top and put it into a wok or heavy saucepan. Reserve the remaining coconut milk for later.

bring the coconut milk to a boil, then reduce the heat and simmer, uncovered, stirring occasionally, until the coconut oil begins to bubble to the surface and the liquid reduces to a quarter of its original volume. Stir in the curry paste and galangal and bring to a boil. Cook over a moderate to high heat until most of the liquid evaporates.

peel the shrimp and remove the dark vein running along the back. Rinse under cold running water, pat dry on paper towels and add to the mixture in the pan. Stir-fry for 3–4 minutes until the shrimp have turned pink and are cooked through.

stir in the remaining coconut milk and the nam pla and simmer for 6–8 minutes, stirring occasionally.

serve garnished with lime leaves and shredded basil leaves, accompanied by boiled rice, if desired.

Serves 4–6
Preparation time: *10 minutes, plus chilling*
Cooking time: *30–35 minutes*

Braised Chive Flowers with Shrimp

1 tablespoon peanut oil

2 garlic cloves, crushed

6 oz flowering chives, large chives, or scallions, cut into 3 inch lengths

1 tablespoon nam pla (fish sauce)

3 tablespoons dark soy sauce

2 tablespoons superfine sugar

8 oz raw small shrimp, peeled and roughly chopped

1 fresh red chili, sliced, to garnish

boiled jasmine (fragrant) rice, to serve

heat the oil in a wok or large skillet and stir-fry the garlic over a moderate heat for 1 minute. Add the chives or scallions, nam pla, soy sauce, and sugar and stir-fry for a further minute.

add the shrimp to the pan and stir-fry for 3 minutes until they have turned pink and are cooked through. Serve immediately, garnished with sliced red chili and accompanied by boiled jasmine rice.

Serves 3–4
Preparation time: *10 minutes*
Cooking time: *5 minutes*

clipboard: Thai jasmine rice, sometimes known as fragrant rice, is more expensive than other types of long-grain rice, but it is so delicious that it is well worth paying extra for it. If you cook a lot of Asian food, you might even consider buying an 11 lb or 22 lb sack from an Asian market, because this is the most economical way of buying it and it will keep for a year or more.

Mussels with Thai Herbs

The fresh, aromatic herbs combine perfectly with the meaty flesh of the mussels in this dish. Serve with jasmine (fragrant) rice or plain boiled rice to soak up the juices.

4 lb live mussels

5 cups water

6 kaffir lime leaves or ½ teaspoon grated lime zest

zest of 1 lemon

2 lemon grass stalks

1 tablespoon salt

3 fresh red chilies, sliced

3 scallions, chopped

cilantro leaves, to garnish

boiled rice, to serve

wash the mussels in cold water and scrape away any barnacles with a sharp knife. Remove the beards, then allow the mussels to soak in cold water for about 1 hour. Drain and tap any open shells to make sure that they close. Discard any mussels that remain open.

pour the measurement water into a large saucepan and bring to a boil. Add the lime leaves or lime zest, lemon zest, lemon grass, and salt. Then add the mussels, cover and return to a boil.

cook the mussels, shaking the pan occasionally, until they have opened. Drain, reserving half the cooking liquid. Transfer the mussels to a deep serving dish, discarding any that remain closed.

strain the reserved stock, discarding the lime leaves or lime zest, lemon zest and lemon grass. Bring to a boil, add the chilies and scallions and boil vigorously for 2 minutes. Pour over the mussels. Serve immediately, garnished with cilantro and accompanied by boiled rice.

Serves 4
Preparation time: *20 minutes, plus soaking*
Cooking time: *20 minutes*

Rice and Noodles

Coconut Rice

Basmati rice actually comes from India, but it is the ideal accompaniment for most Thai dishes if jasmine (fragrant) rice is not available.

1¾ cups coconut milk

½ teaspoon ground turmeric

1½ cups basmati rice, washed and drained

8 small onions, roughly chopped

20 black peppercorns

1 teaspoon salt

To garnish

fine strips of scallion

slivers of toasted fresh coconut (optional)

put the coconut milk in a saucepan, stir in the turmeric, then add the rice. Bring to a boil, then reduce the heat, cover and simmer gently for about 10 minutes.

add the onions, peppercorns, and salt to the pan and simmer gently for an additional 10 minutes, or until the rice is tender. Be careful not to allow the rice to burn.

transfer to a warm serving dish and garnish with fine strips of scallion and slivers of toasted fresh coconut, if desired.

Serves 4
Preparation time: *10 minutes*
Cooking time: *25 minutes*

Spicy Fried Rice

The quantity of boiled rice needed in this recipe is based on a quantity of about 1 cup raw rice.

4 oz ground beef

8 oz can red kidney beans, drained

1½ tablespoons nam pla (fish sauce), or to taste

1 tablespoon dark soy sauce

4 fresh red chilies, seeded and finely chopped

3 garlic cloves, crushed

½ teaspoon salt

2 tablespoons vegetable oil

10 green beans, trimmed and cut into ½ inch lengths

4½ cups cold boiled rice

1 tablespoon palm sugar or light brown sugar

4 tablespoons roughly chopped basil

salt and pepper (optional)

finely chopped red bell pepper, to garnish

put the ground beef and kidney beans in a bowl. Mix well and then stir in the nam pla and soy sauce. Cover and allow to stand for 30 minutes to let the different flavors blend.

mix the chilies, garlic, and salt together in a separate bowl. Heat the oil in a wok or large skillet and stir-fry the chili mixture over a moderately high heat for 1 minute.

add the beef and kidney bean mixture to the pan and stir-fry for 3 minutes, or until the beef is lightly browned. Add the green beans and stir-fry over a moderate heat for an additional 3 minutes.

add the rice and sugar and stir-fry until the rice is hot and all the ingredients are thoroughly mixed. Add salt and pepper or more nam pla to taste, if necessary. Mix in the basil and transfer to a serving dish. Garnish with chopped red bell pepper.

Serves 4
Preparation time: *10 minutes, plus marinating*
Cooking time: *10 minutes*

Curried Rice with Black Fungus

Black fungus are a type of dried mushroom, also known as wood fungus, mouse ear, and cloud ear. They are used in soups and stir-fries as well as in chicken and fish dishes.

4 oz dried black fungus

2 tablespoons peanut oil

I onion, chopped

1½ cups cold boiled rice

I teaspoon curry powder

½ teaspoon soy sauce

2 tomatoes, finely chopped

salt and pepper

I tablespoon Crispy Garlic (see page 250), to garnish

soak the black fungus in several changes of warm water for 15–20 minutes, then drain and slice.

heat the oil in a wok or large skillet over a moderate heat, then add all the ingredients, in turn (add the black fungus after the onion), making sure that the rice is well mixed in.

increase the heat to high and stir-fry for 3–4 minutes. Turn into a bowl, garnish with the crispy garlic, and serve immediately.

Serves 4
Preparation time: *10 minutes, plus soaking*
Cooking time: *5 minutes*

Yellow Rice with Mushrooms

The spice turmeric, a member of the ginger family, gives this dish its yellow color. The roots are ground and dried to give the powder that is widely used in all Asian cooking.

2 tablespoons peanut oil

3 cups cold boiled rice

1 cup snow peas

1¼ cups halved button mushrooms

1 cup canned, drained bamboo shoots

1 teaspoon ground turmeric

2 teaspoons palm sugar or light brown sugar

1 tablespoon soy sauce

1 teaspoon salt

pepper, to taste

To garnish

1 tablespoon Crispy Garlic (see page 250)

1 large fresh red chili, seeded and cut into strips

heat the oil in a wok or large skillet over a moderate heat. Add the rice and stir thoroughly so that it is coated with the oil, then add all the remaining ingredients. Stir-fry over a low heat until thoroughly mixed.

increase the heat and stir-fry for 1–2 minutes, making sure that the rice does not stick to the wok.

turn onto a serving dish, garnish with the crispy garlic and strips of red chili and serve immediately.

Serves 3–4
Preparation time: *3 minutes*
Cooking time: *5 minutes*

Fried Rice with Beans and Tofu

Tofu is made from crushed soybeans, and although usually sold in soft or silken forms, it is also available ready-fried.

about 3 cups peanut oil, for deep-frying

4 oz ready-fried tofu, diced

2 eggs

1½ cups cold boiled rice

3 teaspoons palm sugar or light brown sugar

1½ tablespoons soy sauce

2 teaspoons crushed dried chilies

1 teaspoon vegetarian nam pla (fish sauce) or salt

1 cup fine green beans, finely chopped

½ cup Crispy Mint (see page 248), to garnish

heat the oil in a wok or deep skillet to 350–375°F, or until a cube of bread browns in 30 seconds. Deep-fry the tofu until golden brown on all sides. Remove it with a slotted spoon, drain on paper towels and set aside.

pour off all but 2 tablespoons of the oil from the pan. Heat the oil until hot, then crack the eggs into it, breaking the yolks and stirring around.

add the rice, sugar, soy sauce, crushed dried chilies, and nam pla or salt and increase the heat to high. Stir-fry vigorously for 1 minute.

reduce the heat and add the green beans and tofu. Increase the heat again and stir-fry vigorously for 1 minute. Turn onto a serving dish and serve immediately, garnished with the crispy mint.

Serves 4
Preparation time: *10 minutes*
Cooking time: *about 6 minutes*

Crispy Noodles

Tamarind imparts a slightly sour, tart flavor to foods. If you cannot find the pulp, use tamarind concentrate or lemon juice.

1¼ cups tamarind water (see page 32)

1 cup palm sugar or light brown sugar

5 tablespoons tomato ketchup

3 tablespoons nam pla (fish sauce)

about 3 cups oil, for deep-frying

4 oz dried rice vermicelli, soaked in hot water for 15–20 minutes and drained

1½ oz ready-fried tofu, cut into 1 x ¼ inch pieces

green shoots of 1 scallion, sliced, to garnish

heat the tamarind water and sugar in a wok or large skillet until the sugar dissolves (it will foam up). Add the ketchup and stir for 1 minute, then add the nam pla. Cook, stirring, for 20–25 minutes. The sauce will gradually thicken until it is almost the consistency of jelly and will stick to the noodles. Remove the pan from the heat and allow to cool slightly.

heat the oil in a separate wok or large skillet to 350–375°F, or until a cube of bread browns in 30 seconds. Deep-fry the noodles, a handful at a time, for a few seconds until puffed up. Remove with a slotted spoon and drain on paper towels.

when all the noodles are fried, put them in a large bowl and drizzle the sweet red sauce over them, working it in carefully with your hands until the crispy white noodles turn a pinky-brown. Pour off all but 1 tablespoon of the oil from the pan. Arrange the noodles on a serving dish.

heat the oil and stir-fry the tofu pieces briefly over a moderately high heat, then arrange on top of the noodles. Sprinkle with the sliced scallion shoots and serve immediately.

Serves 4
Preparation time: *10 minutes, plus soaking*
Cooking time: *35 minutes*

Chiang Mai Noodles

6 oz dried egg noodles

1 tablespoon peanut oil

2 garlic cloves, finely chopped

2 tablespoons Red Curry Paste (see page 12)

1/4 teaspoon crushed dried chilies

1 cup coconut milk

2 cups Vegetable Stock (see page 15)

1/4 teaspoon ground turmeric

1 1/2 teaspoons curry powder

2 tablespoons vegetarian nam pla (fish sauce) or soy sauce

1 tablespoon palm sugar or light brown sugar

1 celery stick, chopped

2 tablespoons finely sliced shallot

2 tablespoons chopped red bell pepper

1 oz dried shiitake mushrooms, soaked for 15–20 minutes in warm water, drained and sliced, hard stalks cut away and added to a stockpot

1 tablespoon Crushed Roasted Nuts (see page 248)

To serve

2 tablespoons lime juice, or to taste

1/4 cup each pickled cabbage and shallot

cook the noodles in a saucepan of boiling water for 5–6 minutes. Drain and rinse under cold running water to prevent further cooking.

heat the oil in a wok or large skillet and stir-fry the garlic over a moderate heat for 1 minute, or until golden. Add the curry paste and chilies and mix thoroughly. Pour in the coconut milk, stirring constantly, then bring to a boil and cook until the liquid thickens a little.

add the stock, turmeric, curry powder, nam pla or soy sauce, and sugar and return to a boil. Reduce the heat and add the celery, shallot, red pepper, mushrooms, and nuts. Return to a boil, then remove from the heat.

transfer the noodles to a large serving bowl and pour over the sauce. Sprinkle with the lime juice to taste and serve with the pickled cabbage and shallot.

Serves 4
Preparation time: *30 minutes*
Cooking time: *15 minutes*

Egg Noodles with Oyster Mushrooms

Sometimes known as abalone, oyster mushrooms are fan shaped and pale gray. They have a smooth texture and are widely available in supermarkets.

8 oz dried egg noodles

2 tablespoons peanut oil

3 garlic cloves, chopped

1 teaspoon palm sugar or light brown sugar

1 tablespoon soy sauce

1 tablespoon vegetarian nam pla (fish sauce) or soy sauce

1/2 teaspoon salt, or to taste

2 oz oyster mushrooms, torn into pieces

1/2 onion, chopped

1 cup snow peas

4 large fresh orange chilies, cut into fine strips

pepper (optional)

cook the noodles in a saucepan of boiling water for 5–6 minutes. Drain and rinse under cold running water to prevent further cooking.

heat the oil in a wok or large skillet and stir-fry the garlic briefly, then add the noodles, sugar, soy sauce, nam pla or soy sauce, and salt. Stir-fry vigorously over a high heat for 1 minute.

add the vegetables and chilies and stir-fry for 2–3 minutes, then reduce the heat and taste and adjust the seasoning, if necessary. Turn onto a serving dish and serve immediately.

Serves 4
Preparation time: *5 minutes*
Cooking time: *10–12 minutes*

Noodles with Vegetables

Use peanut oil with this dish rather than a strongly flavored oil like olive oil, which will dominate it.

8 oz dried egg noodles

about 2 tablespoons peanut oil

½ leek, sliced

1 oz oyster mushrooms, torn into pieces

1 celery stick with leaves, chopped

2 cups sliced Chinese cabbage

½ cup cauliflower florets

2 tablespoons soy sauce

1½ tablespoons palm sugar or light brown sugar

½ teaspoon salt, or to taste

1 teaspoon pepper, or to taste

2 tablespoons Crispy Garlic (see page 250)

cilantro leaves, to garnish

cook the noodles in a saucepan of boiling water for 5–6 minutes. Drain and rinse under cold running water to prevent further cooking.

heat the oil in a wok or large skillet over a moderate heat, then add all of the ingredients, in turn, including the noodles, stir-frying briefly after each addition. Stir-fry for 3–4 minutes, adding more oil, if necessary. Taste and adjust the seasoning, if necessary.

transfer to a warm serving dish, garnish with cilantro leaves and serve immediately.

Serves 4
Preparation time: *8 minutes*
Cooking time: *about 10 minutes*

Noodles with Fish Curry Topping

8 oz cod fillets

1 cup water

4 cups coconut milk

3 tablespoons Red Curry Paste (see page 12)

3 tablespoons nam pla (fish sauce)

8 oz dried thick noodles

1 cup green beans

2 cups fresh bean sprouts

½ cup coconut cream

To garnish

1 fresh red chili, seeded and finely sliced

½ cup basil leaves

put the fish in a saucepan with the measurement water and bring to a boil. Reduce the heat and simmer for 8–10 minutes, or until the fish flakes easily when tested with a fork. Remove the fish from the saucepan with a slotted spoon, reserving the stock. Discard the skin and flake the flesh.

transfer the flaked fish to a clean saucepan with the coconut milk. Bring to just below boiling point and stir in the reserved fish stock.

add the curry paste to the fish mixture, together with the nam pla. Simmer for 15 minutes, stirring occasionally.

meanwhile, bring 2 large saucepans of water to a boil. Add the noodles to the first and cook for 10 minutes. For the last 3 minutes of cooking, add the green beans and bean sprouts to the second pan and boil for 2–3 minutes and 1 minute respectively. Drain all 3 ingredients thoroughly, rinse under cold running water and drain again.

with clean hands, carefully scoop the noodles into loose nest shapes, transfer to a large serving plate with the green beans and bean sprouts and warm through in a preheated oven, 325°F.

when the fish curry has thickened and a thin film of oil appears on the surface, stir in the coconut cream. Bring to a boil, then remove from the heat and spoon over the noodles. Serve immediately, with the green beans and bean sprouts, garnished with sliced red chili and basil leaves.

Serves 4
Preparation time: *20 minutes*
Cooking time: *25 minutes*

Rice Vermicelli in Coconut Milk

8 oz dried rice vermicelli

2 teaspoons vegetable oil

2 eggs, beaten

2 cups coconut milk

½ onion, roughly chopped

8 oz raw large shrimp, peeled and deveined

4 tablespoons salted soybean flavoring

2 tablespoons palm sugar or light brown sugar

1 tablespoon lemon juice

5 cups fresh bean sprouts

½ cup chopped scallion, plus very fine strips of scallion to garnish

To garnish

3 tablespoons chopped cilantro leaves

2 fresh red chilies, seeded and cut into fine strips

soak the vermicelli in a bowl of hot water for 15–20 minutes, then drain. Bring a large saucepan of water to a boil, add the vermicelli and cook, stirring occasionally, for 15 minutes. Drain well and set aside.

heat the oil in an omelet pan or small skillet and add the eggs. Tilt the pan to form an omelet, lifting the sides of the omelet to allow any uncooked egg mixture to flow underneath. Remove the cooked, set omelet from the pan and slice it into thin shreds. Keep warm.

pour the coconut milk into a wok or saucepan and bring to a boil. Cook over a high heat for 10 minutes, or until a film of oil forms on the surface. Stir in the onion, shrimp, soybean flavoring, sugar, and lemon juice. Cook for 5 minutes, then transfer half the mixture to a bowl and keep warm.

add the reserved vermicelli to the mixture in the pan. Mix well and cook for 5 minutes. Stir in half the bean sprouts and scallions.

pile the vermicelli mixture onto a serving dish and top with the reserved shrimp mixture and shredded omelet. Garnish with the chopped cilantro, fine strips of red chili, and very fine strips of scallion and serve with the remaining bean sprouts and scallions.

Serves 4
Preparation time: *15 minutes, plus soaking*
Cooking time: *45 minutes*

Fried Rice with Seafood

Fried rice dishes always use rice that has been cooked and left over from a previous meal. This delicious mixture of seafood with fried rice is a typical seaside dish, available all along the coasts of Thailand.

3 tablespoons sunflower oil

4 garlic cloves, finely chopped

1 lb mixed seafood, such as raw peeled shrimp, shelled, cleaned scallops, cleaned squid, and skinned white fish fillet

6 cups cold boiled rice

2 onions, sliced

1 inch fresh gingerroot, peeled and finely sliced

2½ tablespoons soy sauce

3 scallions, finely sliced

To garnish

1 long fresh red or green chili, seeded and finely sliced

cilantro leaves (optional)

heat the oil in a wok or large skillet and stir-fry the garlic over a moderate heat for 1 minute, or until golden.

add the mixed seafood to the pan and stir-fry over a high heat for 1–2 minutes. Add the rice, onions, ginger, and soy sauce and stir-fry for 3–4 minutes. Stir in the scallions.

spoon the mixture onto a serving plate, garnish with the sliced chili and a few cilantro leaves, and serve immediately.

Serves 4
Preparation time: *10 minutes*
Cooking time: *5–7 minutes*

Egg-fried Noodles

This dish might almost be regarded as Thailand's standard noodle recipe. It is quick and easy to prepare and is usually offered as a secondary rather than a main dish.

4 tablespoons peanut oil

I garlic clove, crushed

I shallot or small onion, thinly sliced

4 oz fresh egg noodles

grated zest of I lime

2 teaspoons soy sauce

2 tablespoons lime juice

4 oz boneless, skinless chicken breast or pork tenderloin, sliced

4 oz raw crabmeat or cleaned squid, cut into strips

4 oz raw peeled shrimp

I tablespoon yellow soybean paste

I tablespoon nam pla (fish sauce)

2 tablespoons palm sugar or light brown sugar

2 eggs

2 fresh red chilies, seeded and chopped

pepper

To garnish

cilantro leaves

finely pared lime zest

heat half the oil in a wok or large skillet and stir-fry the garlic and shallot or onion over a moderate heat until soft and golden.

plunge the egg noodles into a saucepan of boiling water and leave to stand for a few seconds. Drain well and then add to the pan. Stir-fry with the grated lime zest, soy sauce, and lime juice for 3–4 minutes. Remove, drain and keep warm.

heat the remaining oil in the pan and stir-fry the chicken or pork, crabmeat or squid, and shrimp over a high heat until cooked through. Season with pepper and stir in the soybean paste, nam pla, and sugar.

break the eggs into the pan and stir gently until the mixture sets. Add the chilies and taste and adjust the seasoning, if necessary. Stir in the noodles and heat through over a low heat. Serve immediately, garnished with cilantro leaves and finely pared lime zest.

Serves 4
Preparation time: *10 minutes*
Cooking time: *20 minutes*

Noodles with Chicken and Shrimp

4 tablespoons vegetable oil

2 garlic cloves, crushed

4 oz cooked fresh or dried egg noodles

2 tablespoons dark soy sauce

4 oz mixed raw sliced boneless, skinless chicken breast and cleaned squid, and whole peeled shrimp

1/2 teaspoon pepper

2 tablespoons nam pla (fish sauce)

2 cups mixed shredded cabbage and broccoli florets

1 1/4 cups Chicken Stock (see page 14)

1 tablespoon cornstarch

2 tablespoons water

2 tablespoons palm sugar or light brown sugar

heat half the oil in a wok or large skillet and stir-fry half the garlic over a moderate heat for 1 minute, or until golden. Add the noodles and half the soy sauce and stir-fry for 3–5 minutes. Transfer to a serving dish and keep warm.

heat the remaining oil in the pan and stir-fry the remaining garlic over a moderate heat for 1 minute, or until golden. Add the chicken breast, squid, shrimp, pepper, and nam pla and stir-fry for 5 minutes.

add the shredded cabbage and broccoli florets to the pan and stir-fry for 3 minutes.

stir in the stock. Blend the cornstarch with the measurement water and stir into the pan. Add the remaining soy sauce and sugar and bring to a boil. Reduce the heat and cook, stirring constantly, for 3 minutes. Pour the thickened sauce over the noodles and serve immediately.

Serves 4
Preparation time: *10 minutes*
Cooking time: *20 minutes*

Fried Noodles with Chicken and Broccoli

1½ tablespoons vegetable oil

1 large garlic clove, chopped

¼ onion, chopped

4 oz boneless, skinless chicken breast, chopped

1 egg

6 oz dried rice vermicelli, soaked in hot water for 15–20 minutes and drained

1½ tablespoons palm sugar or light brown sugar

1 tablespoon tamarind water (see page 32) or distilled white vinegar

5 tablespoons soy sauce

1½ cups broccoli florets and stalks

1 tablespoon chopped red bell pepper

3 scallions, chopped

1 cup fresh bean sprouts

2 tablespoons Crushed Roasted Nuts (see page 248)

½ teaspoon pepper

cilantro leaves, to garnish

heat the oil in a wok or large skillet and stir-fry the garlic, onion, and chicken over a high heat for 2 minutes.

reduce the heat and break the egg into the mixture, stirring constantly. Add the vermicelli, sugar, tamarind water or vinegar, soy sauce, and broccoli and stir-fry for 2 minutes.

add all the remaining ingredients, increase the heat and stir-fry vigorously for about 2 minutes.

turn the noodle mixture onto a serving dish, garnish with cilantro leaves and serve immediately.

Serves 4
Preparation time: *10 minutes, plus soaking*
Cooking time: *6–7 minutes*

Vermicelli Noodles with Sauce

Although fresh gingerroot is a good substitute if you cannot find galangal, never use dried ground ginger in Thai dishes.

1 lb dried rice vermicelli

4 oz ready-fried tofu, sliced, plus extra to garnish

1 tablespoon Red Curry Paste (see page 12)

2 oz fresh galangal or gingerroot, peeled and chopped

1 cup coconut milk

1½ teaspoons salt

1¼ cups hot water

2 teaspoons palm sugar or light brown sugar

To garnish

cilantro leaves

1 fresh red chili, finely sliced

soak the vermicelli in a bowl of hot water for 15–20 minutes.

meanwhile, put the tofu, curry paste, galangal or ginger, coconut milk, and salt in a food processor and process until smooth. Add the measurement hot water and process again for 5 seconds.

pour the blended mixture into a saucepan and bring to a boil, stirring constantly. Reduce the heat to a simmer and add the sugar. Cook gently for a further 3–4 minutes.

drain the vermicelli and transfer to a warm serving bowl. Pour over the sauce and garnish with chopped cilantro, tofu slices, and sliced red chili. Serve immediately.

Serves 4–6
Preparation time: *10 minutes, plus soaking*
Cooking time: *about 10 minutes*

Noodle Salad

For a hotter version of this popular dish, add five small bird's eye chilies to the sauce.

7 oz dried thick noodles

Fish balls

10 oz cod fillets, cooked, skinned, and flaked

1 tablespoon Red Curry Paste (see page 12)

1 tablespoon chopped cilantro leaves, plus an extra sprig to garnish

1 teaspoon salt

1 tablespoon water

1 cup coconut milk

4 tablespoons nam pla (fish sauce)

4 heaping teaspoons palm sugar or light brown sugar

To garnish

1/3 red, 1/3 yellow, and 1/3 green bell pepper, cored, seeded, and sliced into fine strips

1 tablespoon finely sliced fresh gingerroot

To serve

2 inch piece of fresh gingerroot, peeled and finely sliced

3 garlic cloves, finely sliced

2 tablespoons ground dried shrimp

bring a large saucepan of water to a boil, add the noodles and cook for 10 minutes. Drain thoroughly, rinse under cold running water and drain again. With clean hands, carefully scoop the noodles into loose nest shapes, transfer to a large serving plate and warm through in a preheated oven, 325°F.

make the fish balls. Mix the cod, curry paste, chopped cilantro, salt, and measurement water together in a bowl. Form the mixture into 40 balls and set aside.

bring the coconut milk to a boil in a medium saucepan and add the fish balls, a few at a time, so that the milk continues to boil. Cook for about 4–5 minutes, turning over halfway through the cooking time. As each ball cooks, remove it with a slotted spoon and drain on a wire rack set over a tray. Allow to cool. Reserve the coconut milk.

arrange the cooked fish balls on top of the noodles and sprinkle with the ginger, garlic, and ground dried shrimp. Combine the reserved coconut milk with the nam pla and sugar. Pour the spiced milk over the top of the fish balls and garnish with fine strips of red, yellow, and green bell pepper, finely sliced ginger, and a cilantro sprig. Serve immediately.

Serves 4
Preparation time: *10 minutes*
Cooking time: *25 minutes*

Desserts

Fresh Fruit Platter

Desserts are not routinely offered after a Thai meal, but a fresh fruit salad is always welcome. Use whatever fruits are in season.

2 ripe mangoes

I small ripe papaya

I½ cups fresh litchis

I slice of watermelon

I lime, cut into quarters

peel and thickly slice the mangoes, discarding the seeds. Peel the papaya, scoop out the seeds and cut the flesh into 4 or 8 pieces.

peel the litchis and remove the seeds. Peel the watermelon and cut the flesh into chunks, removing as many of the seeds as you can.

arrange the fruit on a serving plate, with the lime quarters ready to squeeze over the papaya.

Serves 4

Preparation time: *15–20 minutes*

Bananas in Coconut Milk

Thai cooks can choose between more than 20 varieties of banana, but in the West most food stores offer only two. If possible, use small, sweet fruits, rather than the larger, blander type.

¾ cup coconut milk

½ cup water

3 tablespoons palm sugar or light brown sugar

1 large or 2 small bananas, peeled, halved lengthwise and each half cut into 4 pieces

put the coconut milk, measurement water, and sugar in a saucepan and simmer, stirring occasionally, for about 6 minutes.

add the bananas and cook for 4 minutes, or until heated through. Serve the bananas hot or cold with the milk poured around them.

Serves 4
Preparation time: *2 minutes*
Cooking time: *10 minutes*

Coconut Balls

In Thailand, cooks often add food coloring to this mixture to jazz up the appearance a little. Yellow and pink are popular.

1¼ cups water

1½ cups palm sugar or light brown sugar

3 cups grated fresh coconut or shredded coconut, softened with a little cold water

mint sprigs, to decorate

put the measurement water and sugar in a saucepan and bring to a boil, stirring, until the sugar dissolves. Boil, without stirring, for 5 minutes, or until a thick sugar syrup forms. Add the coconut and continue boiling until the syrup has almost all evaporated.

put 12 tablespoonfuls of the mixture on a baking sheet, shaping each spoonful into a ball as you go.

allow to cool and harden for about 1½ hours. Serve in bowls, decorated with mint sprigs.

Makes 12
Preparation time: *15 minutes, plus cooling and setting*
Cooking time: *20 minutes*

Mango and Sticky Rice

Sticky rice, sometimes called glutinous rice, is a type of short-grain rice used in many Thai desserts. It must be soaked before use and then steamed, never boiled.

2½ cups sticky (glutinous) rice

¾ cup palm sugar or light brown sugar

1¼ cups coconut milk

2 ripe mangoes

soak the rice for at least 6 hours or overnight. Drain and rinse the rice well, then cook in a steamer for about 30 minutes. Give the rice a good shake halfway through steaming to make sure that it is evenly cooked.

meanwhile, combine the sugar and coconut milk in a large bowl and stir well.

when the rice is cooked, transfer it to the coconut mixture and stir thoroughly for 2–3 minutes to achieve a creamy consistency. Cover with a lid and leave to stand at room temperature for 30 minutes.

peel and slice the mangoes, discarding the seeds, and serve arranged attractively on a dish with the rice.

Serves 4
Preparation time: *10 minutes, plus soaking and standing*
Cooking time: *30 minutes*

Banana Fritters

You could serve the fritters with ice cream, but a more traditional accompaniment would be a caramel sauce made with palm sugar, water, and a little coconut milk.

about 3 cups peanut oil, for deep-frying

1½ lb bananas (about 5)

superfine sugar, to serve

Batter

¾ cup water

1¼ cups rice flour or all-purpose flour

1½ cups grated fresh coconut or shredded coconut

½ teaspoon salt

6 tablespoons palm sugar or light brown sugar

1 egg

make the batter. Beat all the batter ingredients together in a bowl.

heat the oil in a wok or deep skillet to 350–375°F, or until a cube of bread browns in 30 seconds. Meanwhile, peel the bananas, cut each one lengthwise into thirds, then cut each third crosswise to make slices about 3 inches long.

coat the banana slices with the batter and slide them carefully into the hot oil, 3 or 4 at a time. Deep-fry for 3–4 minutes until golden brown. Remove with a slotted spoon and drain on paper towels.

when all the banana slices are cooked, arrange them on a serving dish and sprinkle with superfine sugar. Serve immediately.

Serves 4
Preparation time: *8 minutes*
Cooking time: *about 10 minutes*

Coconut Cream Custard

Using bowls made from banana leaves would be a spectacular way of serving this dessert, but if you are afraid that the bowls might leak, use ramekins wrapped in banana leaves and tied with string.

2 large eggs

¾ cup coconut milk

¾ cup palm sugar or light brown sugar

¼ teaspoon salt

2 banana leaves, formed into 4 bowls (optional)

shredded coconut or grated fresh coconut, to decorate

beat the eggs in a bowl. Add the coconut milk and sugar and beat well, then add the salt and beat again.

pour the mixture into 4 ramekins or, if you prefer, into banana leaf bowls. Transfer the filled ramekins or banana leaf bowls to a steamer and steam for 15–20 minutes.

serve warm, decorated with shredded or grated coconut.

Serves 4
Preparation time: *5 minutes*
Cooking time: *15–20 minutes*

Mung Bean Balls in Syrup

¾ cup shelled split mung beans

8 cups water

1 cup coconut milk

4 cups palm sugar or light brown sugar

1 teaspoon vanilla extract

20 egg yolks, lightly beaten

To decorate

confectioners' sugar

nasturtiums, pansies, or other edible flower petals

wash the beans under cold running water until the water runs clear. Transfer the beans to a large saucepan, add 6 cups of the measurement water and bring to a boil. Reduce the heat and simmer for 20 minutes.

drain the beans thoroughly and return them to a clean saucepan with the coconut milk and ¾ cup of the sugar.

cook the mixture over a low heat, stirring constantly, until it is thick and dry enough to be shaped. To test if the mixture is the right consistency, remove it from the heat, allow to cool slightly, then prod gently with a clean finger. If the mixture does not stick to your finger, it is ready. Beat in the vanilla extract and allow to cool.

when the mixture is cold, form it into ovals, about ½–1 inch long, and set aside.

put the remaining measurement water in a large saucepan with the remaining sugar and bring to a boil, stirring, until all the sugar dissolves. Boil, without stirring, for 5 minutes.

remove the sugar syrup from the heat. Dip the mung bean balls in the beaten egg yolks, then add them to the syrup. When the surface of the syrup is covered with coated balls, return the pan to the heat and bring the syrup to a boil. Boil for 5 minutes, turning the balls over halfway through cooking. When the balls are cooked, transfer to a serving dish with a slotted spoon. Repeat until all the balls are cooked. Serve hot or cold, sprinkled with confectioners' sugar and scattered with edible flower petals.

Serves 4
Preparation time: *15 minutes, plus cooling*
Cooking time: *45 minutes*

Golden Threads in Syrup

1 egg

11 egg yolks

2 cups water

3½ cups palm sugar or light brown sugar

To serve

diced dried papaya

mint sprigs

finely grated fresh coconut (optional)

mix the egg and egg yolks together in a large bowl. Beat with a hand-held electric mixer or a wire beater until frothy, then strain into a large pitcher.

combine the measurement water and sugar in a saucepan and bring to a boil, stirring until the sugar dissolves. Boil, without stirring, for 5 minutes.

make the threads. Fill a plastic pastry bag fitted with a fine writing tip with the egg mixture, or use a waxed paper cone with the very tip snipped off, and block the nozzle or hole with your fingertip. Hold it over the boiling syrup, remove your finger and drizzle the egg mixture into the syrup using a spiral movement in one direction only. Try not to break the thread. As soon as the threads are cooked (they cook very quickly), remove with a slotted spoon and drain on paper towels.

repeat with the remaining egg mixture, adding a little water if the syrup becomes too thick.

serve immediately with the diced dried papaya and mint sprigs, topped with grated coconut, if desired.

Serves 4
Preparation time: *5 minutes*
Cooking time: *10 minutes*

Fried Apple and Coconut Cakes

You can prevent the apple rings from turning brown while you work by dropping them into a bowl of acidulated water. Pat them dry on paper towels before adding them to the batter.

½ cup palm sugar or light brown sugar

2 cups water

2½ cups rice flour

1 egg

2 teaspoons baking powder

pinch of salt

1½ cups grated fresh coconut or shredded coconut

4 apples

oil, for deep-frying

confectioners' sugar, to decorate

crème fraîche or plain yogurt, to serve

put the sugar and measurement water in a saucepan and heat over a low heat, stirring constantly, until the sugar dissolves. Bring to a boil, then stir gently for 2–3 minutes until syrupy. Remove from the heat and allow to cool.

mix together the flour, egg, baking powder, salt, and coconut in a large bowl to form a smooth paste.

pour the cooled syrup into the flour paste mixture and beat to form a smooth batter. Cover and allow to stand for 20 minutes.

core the apples and cut them into rings. Add to the batter.

heat the oil in a wok or deep skillet to 350–375°F, or until a cube of bread browns in 30 seconds. Deep-fry the apple rings, in batches, until golden brown on both sides, turning once. Remove with a slotted spoon and drain on paper towels.

dust the apple rings with confectioners' sugar and serve hot with crème fraîche or yogurt.

Serves 4
Preparation time: *20 minutes, plus cooling and standing*
Cooking time: *about 15 minutes*

Silom Sunrise

If you are planning a special dinner party, make it go with an extra swing by offering your guests this delicious drink.

2 ripe mangoes, peeled, seeded, and sliced

½ cup tequila

3 tablespoons Triple Sec

1½ tablespoons grenadine

⅓ cup lime or lemon juice

⅓ cup sugar syrup

6 ice cubes, crushed

lime or lemon slices, to serve

put all the ingredients in a blender and blend until the ice is crushed.

serve in pretty glasses, decorated with lime or lemon slices.

Serves 4
Preparation time: *10–12 minutes*

clipboard: Although you can get canned and dried mangoes, use fresh, ripe fruits for this recipe. Cut the mangoes lengthwise either side of the large, flat seed before you slice the flesh.

Sauces and Garnishes

Lime and Fish Sauce

6 tablespoons lime juice

2 teaspoons palm sugar or light brown sugar

½–1 teaspoon nam pla (fish sauce)

½ teaspoon finely chopped shallot

1 teaspoon finely chopped fresh red chili

squeeze the lime juice into a small bowl and add the sugar. Mix well until the sugar dissolves.

add the remaining ingredients and serve as a dipping sauce.

Preparation time: *4–5 minutes*

Hot Sweet Sauce

½ cup distilled white vinegar or Chinese rice vinegar

⅓ cup palm sugar or light brown sugar

¼ teaspoon salt

1 small fresh green chili, finely chopped

1 small fresh red chili, finely chopped

pour the vinegar into a small saucepan and heat over a low heat. Add the sugar and salt and cook, stirring, until the sugar dissolves. Remove from the heat and allow to cool.

pour the sauce into a small bowl and stir in the chopped chilies.

Preparation time: *2 minutes*
Cooking time: *1–2 minutes*

Crispy Basil and Crispy Mint

2 tablespoons peanut oil

½ cup basil or mint leaves

1 small fresh red chili, finely sliced

heat the oil in a wok or large skillet and stir-fry the herb leaves and chili over a moderately high heat for 1 minute until crispy. Remove with a slotted spoon and drain on paper towels.

Preparation time: *2 minutes*
Cooking time: *1 minute*

Crushed Roasted Nuts

3 tablespoons unroasted, unsalted peanuts or cashew nuts

dry-fry the nuts in a skillet, using no oil, stirring constantly, until golden brown. Remove from the heat and allow to cool.

put the nuts in a plastic bag and use a rolling pin to break them into small pieces.

Preparation time: *2 minutes*
Cooking time: *3–5 minutes*

Ground Roast Rice

2 tablespoons uncooked rice

dry-fry the rice in a skillet, using no oil, shaking and stirring constantly, until golden brown. Remove from the heat and allow to cool.

grind the rice in a clean coffee or spice grinder or in a mortar with a pestle.

Preparation time: *2 minutes*
Cooking time: *3–5 minutes*

Garlic Oil

4 tablespoons vegetable or sunflower oil

1 tablespoon crushed garlic

heat the oil in a small skillet and add the crushed garlic.

cook over a low heat, stirring occasionally, until the garlic is golden. Use in recipes as required.

Garlic Mixture

2 tablespoons crushed garlic

2 tablespoons chopped cilantro root or stalk

1/2 tablespoon pepper

put all the ingredients in a mortar and pound with a pestle to a paste.

Crispy Garlic and Crispy Shallots

about 3 cups peanut oil, for deep-frying

2 tablespoons finely chopped garlic

2 tablespoons finely chopped shallots

heat the oil in a wok or large skillet and stir-fry the garlic over a moderately high heat for about 40 seconds until golden.

remove the garlic with a slotted spoon, draining as much oil as possible back into the wok, then spread out on paper towels to drain. Repeat with the shallots, stir-frying for 1½–2 minutes.

when the garlic and shallots are dried and crispy, you can store them in separate airtight containers, where they will keep for up to 1 month. When the oil is cold, return it to an airtight container, to be reused.

Preparation time: *5 minutes*
Cooking time: *2–3 minutes*

Index

Acknowledgments

Main photography © Octopus Publishing Group Limited/Sandra Lane.

Other photography:
Octopus Publishing Group Limited/David Loftus 97, 153, 183; /Neil Mersh 41, 43, 101, 125, 155, 169, 179, 181, 215, 241; /Peter Myers 47, 49, 73, 91, 93, 135, 137, 139, 143, 161, 163, 167, 173, 177, 207, 221, 239; /William Reavell 12, 16, 18, 53, 149 bottom right, 149 top left, 211; /Philip Webb 51.

Executive Editor **Nicky Hill**
Editor **Jessica Cowie**
Executive Art Editor **Darren Southern**
Designer **'ome design**
Picture Researcher **Sophie Delpech**
Senior Production Controller **Martin Croshaw**